Thomas Wolfe Undergraduate

Richard Walser

Thomas Wolfe Undergraduate

"These were the golden years"
—*Look Homeward, Angel*

Durham, N.C.
Duke University Press
1 9 7 7

© 1977, Duke University Press

L.C.C. card no. 77–74768

I.S.B.N. 0–8223–0387–6

Printed in the United States of
America by Heritage Printers, Inc.

Grateful appreciation is hereby extended to Paul Gitlin, Administrator, C.T.A., of the Estate of Thomas Wolfe, 7 West 51 Street, New York, N. Y. 10019, for the privilege of publishing materials from the Thomas Wolfe Collection of William B. Wisdom at Harvard University, by permission of the Houghton Library, and from the Thomas Wolfe Collection in the North Carolina Collection of the University of North Carolina Library at Chapel Hill; and to Fred Wolfe, 723 Otis Boulevard, Spartanburg, S. C. 29302, for permission to quote excerpts from previously unpublished letters by members of the Wolfe family in the Thomas Wolfe Collection at Chapel Hill.

Contents

Illustrations

Thomas Wolfe Undergraduate

1. Freshman

In the first paragraph of *Look Homeward, Angel*, Thomas Wolfe writes of "that dark miracle of chance which makes new magic in a dusty world." And it was a strange miracle of chance which led him, in the early autumn days of 1916, from his home in Asheville to the campus of the University of North Carolina at Chapel Hill, and it was this same miracle of chance which eventually, during his four years there, made new magic in what had oftentimes been for him a dusty world.

But no wheel of chance, certainly, had determined that he enroll at a college or university as yet undecided. His record under J. M. and Margaret Roberts at the preparatory North State Fitting School in Asheville had ordained that Wolfe not discontinue an education already so propitiously underway. The boy's father, William Oliver Wolfe, an untutored stonecutter who loved poetry and oratory, who felt cheated of a career his inborn talents might have earned him, saw in his son the ultimate realization of his own passions: the boy would be given the best legal education possible and one day become governor of the state. W. O. believed there was ample evidence to support such a lofty aspiration.

Wolfe had always done well in school. He was an early, insatiable reader, and went through his father's home library summarily: Defoe, Dumas, Kipling, O. Henry, the *Oxford Book of English Verse*, and whatever else was on the bookshelf. After lunch he would go to the public library and, according to his mother, return with as many books as he was allowed, and curl up on the sofa to read away the afternoon.[1] At the age of twelve he won a spelling contest against representatives from other western North Carolina schools.[2] From Mrs. Roberts he began to learn a few of the more subtle aspects of English poetry, and was one of four students studying Greek under her husband.[3] Latin came easily to him, as did German.[4] More significant in W. O.'s plans was a gold medal presented his son on May 31, 1916, during graduation exercises at the Fitting School. Young Wolfe, representing the negative, was declared "the best speaker" in a debate on whether "the United States should greatly enlarge its navy."[5] The following evening he won the declamation contest at the school with a speech on "Shakespeare the Man," then rounded off the occasion by collecting a medal for the best essay on Shakespeare.[6] (The year 1916 was the tercentenary of Shakespeare's death.) When Wolfe graduated from the Fitting School in the spring of that year, he was fifteen years old.

Since the three older brothers Frank, Ben, and Fred, had exhibited no talents thought necessary for success at the bar, his father's hopes lay in the youngest son. "My father had eye on the law—The thing to do in the South," Wolfe later noted in his Autobiographical Outline. "Way to politics and public fame . . . To be great in one's town—at most in one's State."[7] As early as May, Emory University wrote Wolfe of having been "advised that you are interested in Law," and expressed a wish that he would consider the Lamar School of Law there.[8] But no out-of-state institution would do, especially after W. O. and Wolfe's sister Mabel, both strong advocates of the University at Chapel Hill, called in Mark Brown, graduate of the University of Tennessee, who had regrets, he said, that he had crossed the state line for an education.[9] The statement so impressed W. O. that he concluded that only at Chapel Hill would his son become acquainted with those who in the future would "stand him in good stead when he comes back to Asheville to practice law. . . . And that will help him a lot, yes, sir, a lot!"[10] In his enthusiasm, he promised to pay for all the boy's expenses at the state university.

Meanwhile, Wolfe had set his mind on Princeton.[11] When Mrs. Wolfe was told of the exorbitant costs at Princeton, she forthwith vetoed her son's first choice. Mrs. Roberts then argued for the University of Virginia, for she was convinced that it was far superior to the University of North Carolina.[12] As the family discussion continued on Spruce Street—in the heated and boisterous way of all Wolfe family discussions— applications were sent out to both institutions. But prodded by Mabel, who had her own private reasons, W. O. was adamant concerning Chapel Hill. Though a Republican and a native of Pennsylvania, he loved North Carolina and identified himself with its determination to emerge from what he believed to be the outrageous years of a malicious Reconstruction perpetrated on the state by vindictive Yankees. "No, you are not going to patronize Virginia," he told his son. "You're a North Carolinian and you'll go to North Carolina. . . . Go to work if you don't go to North Carolina." The boy's practical mother counseled him to approve his father's plan. "After all, Papa is going to pay for it so you take my advice— go this year and it won't be hard to change next year."[13]

Wolfe did not wish to go to Chapel Hill and was still not persuaded. In the quandary, an alternate plan was briefly considered. Early in the summer Mabel had married Ralph Wheaton, salesman for the National Cash Register Company, and the two had moved to Raleigh, not far from Chapel Hill but across the state from Asheville. For the family-centered Mabel, marriage did not compensate for loss of home and brothers. In early August, from an eastern North Carolina town where she was traveling with her husband, she wrote her brother Fred: "Either you, Ben or Tom must come to Raleigh and stay. You and Tom could go to A and M [College] or Ben could get a position. Anything so that I have some one to live with. We want to go to house-keeping but can't as Ralph will be away over half the time and I can't stay alone. Talk Tom into it. . . ."[14] Shortly afterwards, Mabel was back on a visit to Asheville and pressed the point with her youngest brother. Eager to please her, Wolfe wrote a post-card to Ralph in Raleigh: "Ralph, whenever you are not so busy, would you please make some inquiries and find if Raleigh has any good preparatory schools?"[15] Perhaps he was thinking of the time when Mr. and Mrs. Roberts had urged him to return to the Fitting School for another year to work on "his weak subjects"[16]—one of them mathematics, perhaps? Raleigh, it was quickly discovered, had no suitable preparatory school, and now more than ever, Mabel wanted her college-bound brother at nearby Chapel Hill. Edgar R. Rankin of the university staff was in Asheville and met with the family to conclude the matter once and for all,[17] but Wolfe silently retained an option.

Then, when no word came that he had been accepted at the University of Virginia, he reluctantly gave in on September 6 to the family decision—a mere six days before the University of North Carolina opened. On September 8 a letter arrived from Charlottesville directing him to come on there,[18] but it was too late, even if he had been able to change the family's choice. In the dusty world of Spruce Street, the dark miracle of chance had heedlessly prevailed.

On September 9 W. O. wrote to Ralph: "Tom will leave for Chappel Hill Tuesday 12. I have About given out going with him. I will write the Pres. putting him in his cge. and he will Send me the bill for this first half Session."[19] So on that Tuesday, the first day of registration at the University,[20] Wolfe, dressed neatly in a Biltmore homespun suit,[21] took the early-morning train from Asheville and arrived at Durham in late afternoon. There he was met by Ralph, who had motored over from Raleigh, and was driven the twelve miles to Chapel Hill. Among his first impressions of the village, rusty green in mid September, were the "Sophomores before the P. O." and "The magical campus."[22] A turn to the left off the principal thoroughfare, Franklin Street, then a turn to the right down Cameron Avenue, brought Wolfe and his brother-in-law to the three-story rooming house[23] of Mrs. Mattie Eva Hardee, an Asheville widow, who had a good location, only a block and a half from the west entrance to the campus. Mrs. Hardee charged $15 a month for board, $7.50 for a student's half of a room. Out of his first check from W. O., Wolfe paid her two months in advance—an action he was soon to regret.[24] Yet the food was excellent, and around the table at meal time were familiar Asheville faces. Mrs. Hardee's son Charles was in his second year at the university, and several other Asheville students roomed there.[25] From that first night in Chapel Hill, Wolfe was never a solitary, lost figure among strangers.

The village to which he had come bordered on three sides the leafy university, at whose apex was South Building, facing north down a greensward towards Franklin Street. Flanking South Building on one side was Old East, dating back to 1793, the oldest state university structure in the nation. On the other side was Old West, with simple unadorned lines like its twin across the way. Between them was the Old Well, the students' central gathering place. Smith Hall on the east was balanced on the west by Gerrard Hall, a small auditorium. New East and New West, housing the literary societies on their top floors in a splendor unexpected amid the spartan classrooms and dormitories, provided further symmetry. Swain Hall, the student commons, was at the western end of the road passing in front of South Building. On either side of the pristine tree-filled greensward, improvidently maintained and crisscrossed by footpaths, were university halls old and new, with other buildings fanning out a moment's distance away. The library, with its 75,000 volumes, was semicircled on the north and west by modest fraternity houses, and was conveniently located just off Franklin Street behind the New Dorms—Battle, Vance, and Pettigrew. A rambling building called the University Inn, enlarged from a wooden hotel built for the visit of President James K. Polk in 1847, faced the New Dorms. An old campus it was, compact and quiet and peaceful, weathered by the years and rustically beautiful, and a long, long way from the turmoil of Spruce Street.

Toward the north and east and west beyond the university buildings were the residences of faculty and townspeople gracefully secluded by the all-embracing trees. In contrast, the small business district fronting both sides of Franklin Street possessed little charm. Among the unattractive structures, mostly frame, only four or five were student haunts. On the south side of Franklin Street was the post office, where the young men had their own boxes and gathered in a crush twice a day after the incoming mail was put up. A few doorways west, the Pickwick Theater, providing the only regular entertainment in the village, was the scene of constant pranks. Hardly had Wolfe settled down before the college newspaper reported how, on a clear night as students queued up to buy tickets, "the floods descended and the rains fell" on the long line at the box office. Some practical joker "had carried a sufficient supply of water to the roof of the Pickwick, from whence it naturally returned to a lower level."[26] The drugstores—Eubanks and Patterson Brothers—lay across the street, and there the young men matched coins for chocolate-covered ice cream bars called "black cows." There was a bank, of course, and grocery and clothing establishments. Two jitney operators, C. S. Pendergraft and Jack Sparrow, ran touring cars four times a day to meet the trains in Durham. Pendergraft advertised that he could fill students' wants "with three Cadillacs and two Fords," and would give "Special attention to Club and Fraternity Feeds." At his jitney stand he sold candy, fruit, and tobacco.[27] The village one-man police force was Chief Lacy Bunn Lloyd himself, always threatening to arrest some youthful sinner, but never managing to do so.

Two nights after Wolfe's arrival a meeting was held in Gerrard Hall to acquaint the new men about various university activities. Cheerleader Si Parker led off with a few boastful cheers, junior class president Albert Coates explained the honor system, and Marion Ross spoke of the advantages of joining one of the literary societies. At Bynum Gymnasium the evening was topped off with a reception for the new men.[28]

Most of these new men, not unlike Wolfe himself, came unsophisticated and bright-eyed from the farms and towns of North Carolina. Their values were such as his. Few could afford even the $300 minimum annual expenses, and seven out of ten earned $50 or more of the costs. In the fall of 1916 some 140 sought jobs as waiters in Swain Hall.[29] The difference between Wolfe and a great majority of the eleven hundred students was his favored status as a young man whose father, thinking of a future governor, happily paid all his son's bills.

During those first days Wolfe stood in line to enroll for his courses.[30] The program he had decided to pursue was a continuation of the concentration in classics begun earlier at the Fitting School. In the required course in algebra and trigonometry, taught by John W. Lasley, he felt little involvement, but such was not true of the other three: English, Latin, and Greek.

For a brief period his English instructor was Edgar Willis Turlington, native North Carolinian recently returned to the university from three years in Oxford as a Rhodes scholar. That fall, after a brief stint teaching Latin, he moved to the

Department of English,[31] with Wolfe among his first students. Perhaps he unwisely flaunted a few British affectations in hopes of impressing the yokels in his class; in any case, Wolfe was annoyed by the man, and soon arranged a shift to James Holly Hanford, budding Milton scholar with a doctorate from Harvard. The two became close friends. Hanford assigned the high-minded and saccharine selections in Briggs's textbook of essays on college life, but he was not finicky about theme subjects. Wolfe wrote a paper on Rasputin,[32] and read aloud one titled "Who I Am" before his classmates, who, though the author was apparently unaware of any indecorum in matters of truthful exposition, were distinctly uncomfortable to have him articulate in ungarnished words the everyday life of Spruce Street, expecially W. O.'s cursing and drinking.[33]

His Latin teacher was tall George K. G. Henry, native of Nova Scotia and a convert from mathematics who felt particular kinship with Horace and the comic dramatists. Among the Romans Wolfe was at home, happily eager to spend hour after hour interlining his texts.[34] Though his Latin classmate Paul Green,[35] more than six years older and already sedulously engaged in writing, had two poems in the November issue of the *University Magazine*, Wolfe's mind was more on Cicero than poetry. Cicero's *De Senectute* and *De Amicitia* were to be followed by the first book of Livy, and the year's work rewardingly concluded with a selection of Horace's lively *Odes* and *Epodes*.[36] For Wolfe there were minor difficulties, for when the overmodest Henry passed word that a trivial Roman indelicacy was to be omitted in translation, Wolfe unmindfully read straight ahead to the embarrassment of the lone girl in the class.[37] On another occasion Wolfe's fluctuating trust in professors was seriously jarred when his smooth translation of a Latin text was criticized as being the professional prose of a "jack." He thereupon procured a "pony," recited its jerky sentences in class, and was praised for his studiousness.[38] It was all pretty disheartening. That Wolfe recognized the imperfections of professors earlier than most of the easygoing students of his generation was quickly apparent.[39] Turlington and Henry did not measure up. Only Hanford and his Greek professor, William Stanly Bernard, escaped his censure. Bully Bernard was a special case.

Dutifully, Wolfe went to his classes and showed up at 10:30 in the morning for chapel exercises in Gerrard Hall,[40] where attendance was compulsory, the assigned seats checked by monitors. After hymns and Scripture reading, favored speakers like President Edward Kidder Graham, Dean Marvin H. Stacy, and Professor Emeritus Kemp P. Battle delivered inspirational talks.[41] On Sundays Wolfe went to the Presbyterian Church[42] to hear "Parson" W. D. Moss, who drew in a large congregation of student worshipers with sermons comparing Christianity to athletics.[43]

In the fall of 1916 the air hung gently over campus and village, and the hours were measured out by the deep and powerful monotone of the bell on top of South Building.

Wolfe remembered the advice of senior Marion Ross about joining a literary society, and on Saturday evening, September 23, with thirty-seven other freshmen he reported to the Dialectic Society[44] to seek membership. The Di, as it was known, was composed of students from the western part of the state and appropriately housed in Old West, as was its counterpart, the Philanthropic, in Old East. The purpose of both was to train students in debate and public speaking. The third-floor chambers of the Di were impressive, handsomely furnished with comfortable chairs facing an elegant rostrum for the officers. Around the hall hung portraits of Di members who had made names for themselves in the history of the state and nation.

On this occasion Professor Horace Williams of the Department of Philosophy made his annual opening address, and Wolfe must have listened attentively to the man who was to

have a profound influence upon him during his last two years
as an undergraduate. Then came the ritual of initiation, with
each of the new members required to speak before the as-
sembly. All in good fun, a sophomore arose and parodied a
declamation on some weighty matter, and the freshmen were
instructed to follow his example. Most of the neophytes understood the humor of the occasion, planned to give brief
statements, and sit down. Not so Wolfe, well trained in elocu-
tion at the Fitting School, who embarked solemnly on a
speech lasting twenty-two minutes.[45] After an introduction
Wolfe pointed one by one to the portraits hanging from the
walls, coming finally to that of Zeb B. Vance, like Wolfe born
in the mountains of Buncombe County. Vance was undoubtedly the most beloved politician in the annals of North Carolina, its popular Civil War governor, and Wolfe felt pride, he
said, to find himself in such distinguished company.[46] "I hope
some day," he concluded, "to see my picture on these walls."[47]
The laughter which greeted the pompous statement brought
a scowl to his face, for neither then nor ever was Wolfe in-
sensitive to mockery of his serious endeavors. Present on the
occasion was senior Sam J. Ervin, Jr., who, surprised at such
a long speech from one seemingly so shy, thought to himself
that the young orator was certainly, among those present, the
one most unlikely ever to have his portrait hang upon those
hallowed walls.[48]

The members' laughter following Wolfe's speech was not
unrelated to the strange apparition before them, for he had,
even under the circumstances, held their attention. Wolfe
was already more than six feet in height, and still growing.
His large hands, his enormous feet, his unruly dark brown
hair atop a small head—none of these, somehow, fitted his
slender, awkward beanpole of a body. Like the other students, he ordinarily wore a jacket and tie, but his trousers
rode high up his legs and his coat sleeves stopped long before
reaching his wrists. He was obviously no Tom Brown at Ox-

ford, but a gawky, self-conscious lad who felt considerably quelled by the middle-class student establishment of Fraternity Row and Senior Class. Yet he was lucky in that the dark miracle of chance had led him into the democratic environs of Chapel Hill and not to patrician grounds at Princeton or Charlottesville.

For the moment the rebuff was forgotten. Nine days later he met with three dozen other new students to organize the Freshman Debating Club, unconnected with the Di, and was elected vice president of the group.[49] He was, one may assume, present for the election of freshman class officers a week afterwards,[50] and for the organizational meeting of the Buncombe County Club towards the end of the month.[51]

On October 3 (it was Thomas Wolfe's sixteenth birthday), W. O. wrote his son Fred, encouraging him in a new job he was undertaking. "I will expect you and Tom," he concluded, "to take care of your mother and perhaps even me. . . . Yes I have great hopes for Tom. And I am very proud of him for he talks right and is a hard Student. and if he keeps his head etc and lives he must nessarily [*sic*] Succeed in the end for Tom has good morals. It is the the [*sic*] height of my life's end ambition to see him through College. for Tom has greater ambition and unless I am greately [*sic*] deceived you will be proud one day to call him your brother and it should be the will of the whole family to see that he has money to finish his college career. . . . I am keeping account of every thing and am trying to keep my expenses within $350 a year but I don't think that is hardly possible with the present high prices of everything. . . . I will now close write when you can and with much love and wishing you all the success, I remain your father W. O. Wolfe."[52]

In Chapel Hill, meanwhile, young Wolfe was moving into the mainstream of campus life under the aegis of his Asheville acquaintances. He was one of ten freshmen taken in tow by Charles G. (Buzz) Tennent of Asheville in accordance with a

Y.M.C.A. program which assigned a prominent upperclass-man to see that the new men got settled down. Tennent played basketball, was a member of the Di Society, and managing editor of the student newspaper, the *Tar Heel.* "I knew Tom quite well," Tennent wrote. "I took Tom under wing at Chapel Hill, and got him into a couple of literary or alleged literary fraternities to which I belonged."[53] Hardly a day passed that Wolfe was not in the company of other Asheville students such as Edmund Burdick, Nemo Coleman, and J. Y. Jordan. Buzz Tennent's older brother Raby thought Wolfe seemed more than sixteen years old,[54] for he mixed with the upperclassmen on an equal, man-to-man basis. Along the gravel paths his Asheville friends and counsellors stopped classmates from other sections of the state to introduce Wolfe, and soon he knew almost every man on campus.[55]

During the fall Wolfe's primary extracurricular interest lay in the Saturday-evening meetings of the Di Society, then in the process of modernizing its practices. Secrecy was eliminated from its assemblies, an attempt was being made to streamline its sessions, memberships became selective instead of inclusive, and debate policies were improved.[56] Yet all was not ideal. The recording of fines and the constant election of new officers consumed nearly as many hours as formal debate and oratory. Too often, it seems, the Di was not taken seriously. Absence incurred a 25¢ fine, but not when a member was out of town. If a student wanted neither to attend nor to pay the fine, he simply walked beyond the city limits, and reported he had been "out of town."[57] The scrupulously honest officers of the society concurred in the "truth" of the statement, and the fine was remitted. In spite of such minor nonsense, Wolfe faithfully participated in society affairs. The Di gave him training, then and later during his college years, in formal declamation, different from the informal delivery at the Fitting School. Now the emphasis was on style, on the orderly argument, on the carefully constructed long sentences, on the dictionary search for the effective word—precise, unusual, attention-getting, perhaps startling. These things were important, but the formality of statement was always strictly to be observed. In an eleven-page speech on national preparedness, "Written in 1916, by Tom Wolfe," are these opening sentences: "Mr. President, ladies and gentlemen [were "ladies" present?] and Honorable Judges, we have arrived at a crisis in our national affairs. Democracy stands at the crossroads. . . ." Toward the end of the document, Wolfe opined, "I am opposed to the so-called preparedness program."[58]

The minutes of the Di disclose that on November 4 Wolfe was fined 25¢ "for allowing fees to remain unpaid." Nor had the matter been taken care of a month later.[59]

The second week of November Wolfe's peregrinating inclinations were durably forecast when he moved from Mrs. Hardee's rooming and boarding house. His advance payment was exhausted, the charges were excessive, and he had developed an intense dislike for her son Charles. "He of the little soul and the fat 'Yes' man," Wolfe described him; Wolfe and Lewis B. McBrayer, another Asheville freshman rooming there, had gradually become the objects of Hardee's insolence and pranks. "The disgusting posture of master and slave," Wolfe later wrote of the situation. "My hatred even then of the expected ritual—That which seems imitated from cheap books."[60] Obviously he was unwilling to submit to any freshman-sophomore indignities whatsoever, regardless of how tradition-sanctioned they may have been. It was true that, during his two months at Mrs. Hardee's, the food had been "excellent," he had formed some of his strongest college attachments, and he had even become friendly with the townspeople. Of the Williams family next door, the story is told of how, when Mr. Williams was cranking his automobile, Wolfe would lean from his window and gleefully shout "Coffee Grinder!"[61]

He moved. But where to? Even a few years afterwards, Wolfe could not remember. He stayed, he jotted down, "at a lady's whose name I forget," and then "at Mrs. Dr. Ledbetters [*sic*]."[62] He may have roomed for a while on West Franklin Street, near the home of Professor W. D. Toy.[63]

For meals he probably wound up at Swain Hall, which accommodated six hundred students at $12.50 a month. There the Buncombe County fellows sat with their friends from Iredell County, and usually from this area in the large hall, where acceptable table manners were hardly de rigueur, came the constant, raucous shouting and the biscuit-throwing.[64]

In accordance with his sister Mabel's plan, Wolfe went on several weekends to Raleigh, where the Ralph Wheatons were ensconced at 525 Blount Street,[65] a "polite boarding house" in the fashionable section of town near the Governor's Mansion. On one of his visits he went with Mabel to the home of John Edward O'Donnell, who was Ralph's employer at the state office of the National Cash Register Company. The occasion was a "Sunday night supper," recalls the O'Donnells' son John Burke, twelve years old at the time, who looked upon the tall, slender university student with awe. Wolfe and Mrs. O'Donnell began a lively argument about evolution. As a strict Roman Catholic, she protested that it was absurd and atheistical to believe that human beings sprang from monkeys. With the self-assurance of a college freshman, Wolfe expressed the opposite view with agitated excitement. Later, at the dinner table, Wolfe became faint, arose without excusing himself and, young John Burke in hot pursuit to ascertain the cause of this abrupt behavior, rushed out the front door, and vomited over the banisters. As soon as he recovered, everyone jokingly accounted for the mishap by proclaiming it was due to a hangover from revels the night before.[66]

Just before Thanksgiving Wolfe's father, thinking the boy would be homesick during his first holiday away from home, wrote Mabel to be sure to have him come to Raleigh. But Wolfe had other plans.

By this time, so involved was he in the life of the college that he was determined to go to Richmond for the Thanksgiving Day football game with the University of Virginia. Not since 1905 had the University of North Carolina won its annual game against the institution considered its bitterest rival. Wolfe was with friends on the special train which pulled out on the spur line from nearby Carrboro at 9:30 on Wednesday evening the twenty-ninth, the round-trip fare only $3. Aboard the day coaches, jammed with excited students, janitors, and faculty members, were J. Y. Jordan and James Howell of Asheville, drummers in the fifteen-member band. A scrub on the team had borrowed Wolfe's new overcoat, and he was wearing, with unconcealed pride, the scrub's "old sweater which had a big N. C. on it." [67] After what must have been a sleepless night for most of those riding northward, the train arrived in Richmond the next morning. The Jefferson Hotel, patronized by North Carolinians, was the scene of a band concert. At 1:30, "with ribbons, banners and pennants flying, about 800 Tar Heels, led by the band, marched down Broad Street out to the Park." There in the third quarter, before fourteen thousand spectators, North Carolina's Bill Folger tore around Virginia's right end to score the only touchdown of the game. A triumphant snake dance by the Chapel Hill students "was the sensation of the day." [68] In jubilation, Wolfe and hundreds of his fellows assembled in the Murphy Hotel lobby and later entrained, sleepy-eyed, for Chapel Hill. On Saturday evening, after festivities in Gerrard Hall, with President Graham and Coach T. J. Campbell making "short speeches on Carolina spirit," a torchlight parade, headed by the band and the football team in two wagons, made its way through the town and over to the athletic field, where around a bonfire, "'spiked' by 15 gallons of oil," the celebrants "danced about until they could dance no more and roared out cheers until every throat was in shreds." [69]

This Richmond trip, for Wolfe, was burnished with an unforgettable magic to which he gave expression again and again. Three years later, for example, when the teams next faced each other, he recalled the bewitching journey in an essay "Ye Who Have Been There Only Know," once more experiencing its indelible bright colors.[70]

A magic not so bright, but even more lasting and indelible, came to Wolfe in early December. Accompanied by Charles Kivett and T. C. Black, two older freshmen who roomed at the Tar Heel Tavern near Mrs. Hardee's, he paid a visit to a Durham brothel and a prostitute who called herself Mamie Smith. It was his first sexual experience. "All the passion and the fire,"[71] he later noted of the occasion. With a second visit to her soon afterwards, Wolfe established a pattern followed for the rest of his undergraduate days.[72] During the Christmas vacation in Asheville, where all the family were gathered for the holidays, he slipped down to a cheap hotel to be with a "red-haired woman."[73] It was an adventurous, perhaps a necessary magic, but perforce tawdry and false.

Among the Asheville students on the post-Christmas ride back east, Wolfe remembered Raby Tennent and Dewey Cline,[74] the latter a friend returning to Raleigh, where he was a freshman at North Carolina A. and M. College. Semester examinations came in mid-January, and when grades for the fall were released, it was clear that Wolfe, with a B in English and three C's in mathematics, Latin, and Greek,[75] was only an average student. Of the twenty freshmen making honor grades, only J. L. Cook scored all A's.[76] Edmund Burdick of Asheville and Paul Green, his mature twenty-two years making it possible for him not only to take advanced English but at the same time teach an overflow section of Freshman Composition,[77] tied for third honors. In the spring semester, Wolfe continued the same subjects with the same professors, managing to improve his Latin to a B, but in mathematics he dropped to a D, with no change in the other two.

During the winter he teamed up with James (Stumpy)

Howell, Verne Johnson, and Charles French Toms, Jr., all from Asheville, and rented one of Dr. Kemp P. Battle's two cottages beyond the Arboretum off the eastern fringe of the campus.[78] Howell was a first-year law student, prime yodeler in the glee club,[79] and leader of his own small band. Johnson and Toms were freshmen. Dr. Battle used one of his cottages as an office, and the other he let out to students. Almost hidden in the woods near a stream, it provided, said an earlier occupant, "perfect balance between solitude and society."[80] In spite of the necessity of carrying water from the Battle well for shaving, of gathering stovewood from the nearby grove, and the inconvenience of an outdoor privy, the cottage, with one room for work, and the other with two double-decker beds for sleep, was ideal for study and reading. Hot showers were available only in Bynum Gymnasium. Howell remembered how Wolfe would come down the hill on Friday afternoons, his arms loaded with library books on history and literature, some of those on the required lists but more of those which were not, and read throughout the weekend. Nobody dared disturb him. On weekday evenings, after study, the four of them gathered around the wood stove for a bull session.[81] Howell thought Wolfe's height would make him a good cross-country runner and urged him to go out for the track team, but after several afternoons on the athletic field, Wolfe apathetically gave up. Thereafter he confined his participation in athletics to baseball-catching and horseshoe-pitching, at both of which he was quite adept.

Informal smokers were among the "improvements" promised that year by the Di Society. The first, held on February 3, with sandwiches, punch, cigarettes and cigars in ample supply, was a great success. Every seat in the hall was filled, jokes were told, stories were swapped, and "Sam Ervin recited some choice bits of his delightful poetry."[82] A few weeks later, with John Terry on the committee of judges, Wolfe was given "honorable mention" in a debate on the "regulation of trusts" as preferable "to dissolution of combinations."[83] As a result of his serious forensic efforts, he was eventually named to the Sophomore-Freshman debating team.[84]

Though six years older than Wolfe, John Skally Terry—member of the junior class, vice president of the Di, faithful worker at the Y.M.C.A., active in publications—was like Wolfe in that he was a highly visible man on the campus, for he carried 270 pounds on his 5′ 10″ frame.[85] From his sophomore year on, Terry sought out several of the greenest freshmen available and moved them gradually into his literary and confessional confines, and there Wolfe soon found himself.[86] One of Terry's protégés later wrote to Terry: ". . . you were a real mama to me and Tom and a lot of the other fellows and if it hadn't been for your mothering us I know we wouldn't have got along as well and certainly wouldn't have had as much fun."[87] Fun, indeed, there was. Wolfe recorded that Terry's "laugh came from him in a high, choking explosive scream that set the throat and the enormous belly into jellied tremors. He did have a very rich, a very instant sense of humor."[88] Of the proper social graces Terry was a strong advocate, and whenever he could find space and music at the Y.M.C.A., he clasped the young fellows to his agile corpulence in an effort to teach them to dance. A cartoon shows him waltzing with an awkward freshman and saying, "I'm the belle of the Y."[89] Before allowing his learners on the dance floor at formal balls, he led them to the balcony of the Gym, there to gaze longingly on the swaying figures below. Wolfe was among the learners, a Terry disciple who looked down at the splendor beneath him, his brain filled with "dreams of women."[90]

But Terry was more than protectiveness and motherliness and laughter. He held certain inflexible opinions, and when these sentimental and moral convictions were opposed, he became sarcastic and venomous. President Graham and Parson Moss were his Galahad and St. Paul. If never a Galahad,

Graham was even so an able man who stated the goals of his institution, angled state support for it, and began building the foundations for the great university it was to become. Such matters as these were of course quite beyond freshman Wolfe, whose main contact with Graham was at chapel, where the President spoke of "service and leadership," of abstractions like "university spirit." Wolfe found it difficult, at least when pragmatic thinking pushed aside his romantic notions, to be a man who had "the university spirit" if it meant he should "cheer a good play even if the Virginia half back had to come around our end to make it."[91] Parson Moss was a different sort, a go-getter, a missionary, an indefatigable Gerrard Hall and Y.M.C.A. speaker. He held prayers in the students' rooms, then lingered on for a bull session. Graham's idealism and Moss's down-to-earth religion delighted most of the young men and simply transported Terry, but Wolfe thought he sensed a shallowness beneath the surface enchantment, and a rift between Terry and him, never a serious or permanent one, came as Chapel Hill moved into spring. A concomitant factor, as Wolfe realized more than nine years later, was Terry's "worship of young male virgins" and the shattering of "His love romance [following] the youth's [Wolfe's?] deflowerment at Durham—Afterwards—bitterness."[92] Fortunately for Wolfe, any bitterness with Terry was of brief duration.

The war in Europe, meanwhile, was far away, though in January, a hundred men and ten members of the faculty had gone off to military camp.[93] A month after the United States broke relations with Germany in February, four hundred students reported for "active military training under the new voluntary training scheme," the government promising to provide rifles and a drill sergeant.[94] The number of participants increased after the declaration of war on April 6. For five evenings a week, the group met for drill, but still without guns or uniforms. On May 8 some 125 students were ordered to Camp Oglethorpe, the seniors given diplomas without taking final examinations. Sixteen-year-old Wolfe, underage and ineligible, took no part in all this.[95]

If he felt out of the motion and excitement, he most certainly did not feel slighted when his name appeared among the "members" of the Booloo Club. Instead of the disgrace he believed it to be, his involuntary "membership" was actually a distinction, if a somewhat disparaging one. All those chosen were freshmen whom the sophomores singled out and honored for their "wit and sharply defined personalities."[96] A local rhymster reported that

> Nowhere are Booloos half so great
> > As at Carolina.
> Nowhere the styles as they create,
> > Down at Carolina.
> A "tack," a cane, an old plug hat,
> The gift of gab and the grace to chat,
> Freshmen with these make the Booloo Frat
> > Down at Carolina.[97]

Wolfe qualified. No one who knew him could have doubted his "gift of gab and the grace to chat."

At the annual Sophomore Banquet, the report of the Booloo Committee, with its descriptive listings of several dozen freshmen, later appearing in the *Tar Heel*, was said to be well done, if somewhat sparing. Alongside classmates Bo Ballew (Grand Guardian of the Bung-hole of the Tappa Keg Fraternity; The Mightiest of the Insignificant) and W. E. Ransom (Candidate for All-America of the Gas Gang; His Own Press Agent), Worth Daniels (Novelist-Author of "Who I Am"), Paul Green ("Nuff Sed"), and Stanley Travis (Grand Protector of the Chips), Wolfe was identified by the phrase "When my picture hangs in the Di."[98] A dozen years later, as Wolfe looked back on his freshman days, he wrote, obviously in a mood for leg-pulling misstatement and unbridled exaggeration, that in "my first year at Chapel Hill . . . I made history. It was I who made the speech of acceptance when elected to the Literary Society, I took the catalogue exam, went to Chapel Saturday and let a Sophomore lead me in prayer at noon. I made half the places on the Booloo Club that year."[99]

Yet there is no escaping the fact that Wolfe felt humiliated, however inoffensive the ascription. Condoning even the gentlest criticism and censure was never his forte. His word for the portrait-hanging episode at "The Freshman Frat," as he called the Di Society, was "Degradation."[100] By spring the slightest unpleasantness racked him with despair.

On her visit to Raleigh and Chapel Hill, Mrs. Wolfe was introduced to a number of her son's friends who, in the manner of polite young gentlemen, told her they would like to visit Asheville in the summer. Ever the businesswoman, Mrs. Wolfe said for them to come along, and if they would drum up some paying guests for her Old Kentucky Home, they might get their board free. She reminded her son to pass around business cards proclaiming the advantages of her rooming house. Though Mabel Wheaton assured the students that they would always be welcome at her brother Tom's home in Asheville,[101] Wolfe was horrified. Back in Raleigh, he stuttered excitedly, "I tell you, M-M-Mabel, Mama's just r-r-r-ruining me over at Chapel Hill."[102]

About this time, for these reasons and others, Wolfe began to withdraw. He continued his trips to the bawdy houses in Durham[103] and Raleigh, but alone. He grew careless of his appearance. He was rapidly growing taller, and of course his clothes more and more became too small for him. His hat had holes in it, and there were the baggy trousers, the twisted tie, the soiled collar, the uncombed hair.[104] Laundries he avoided, and when some piece of clothing was no longer tolerable, he entered whatever store was convenient and purchased a replacement. His mother recalled one occasion when he came to Asheville with thirty shirts ready for washing. At other times she would say, "Tom, you must have some new clothes and a new hat. Those things are not really decent looking to be seen on the street."[105] When a friend like William T. Polk, editor of the *Tar Heel*, urged him to improve his appearance,[106] he paid no attention to the advice, but assumed rather an attitude of indifference, comforted by the self-assurance that he had more important things to do.

The new magic had temporarily lost its brightness, and as his injured sensibilities evolved into a mild but painful paranoia, Wolfe sought a physical separation which he believed would be salutary. "Removal by myself," he wrote.[107] Down in Battle Park, he packed his few belongings, gathered up his textbooks, and moved to a bare, cheerless room above Eubanks Drug Store on Franklin Street. Perhaps the horseplay and joshing of his friends at the cottage had become unbearable. At the new location Carl Durham, one of the druggists, came to know him well.[108] Among the tradespeople of the business district, Wolfe felt less conspicuous than among the prank-playing students. At sixteen he could not know that his dilemma was not unlike that of all sensitive young men, who for the most part are "persecuted" and "alone," "lost" and "wind grieved." If he looked for perfection in others and could not find it, he could retreat to his own ideal fortress, where his savage pride might lock the door against jokes and poisonous comments, as well as against his aching but unwarranted sense of social inferiority. Yet his retreat to the single room above the drugstore—an unsuccessful alienation, as it turned out—did not remove him from the Asheville group of students with whom he was so closely allied. They kept a tribal and affectionate eye on the one of them so independent, so vulnerable, so different from themselves. Wolfe was "alone" only when he chose to think himself so.

In late April he was among twenty students nominated by the Athletic Council, then in charge of the *Tar Heel*, to become one of the ten associate editors of the campus newspaper.[109] Like the others, Wolfe turned in some copy for inspection by a committee looking for the best writers, but when the positions were announced, Wolfe's name was not among the ten on the list.[110]

In spite of minor defeats like this, to say nothing of his attempted self-ostracism, life was not unbearable. In moments of sheer adolescent exuberance, he was a "racing young boy who leaped into the air"[111] simply because life was ecstatic, for at Chapel Hill, like thousands of students before and after him, he had found a home—composed of an entire campus and an entire village. It was not a divided home as in Asheville, where his father lived on Woodfin Street and his mother on Spruce. To replace the disorder of Asheville, he settled into a casual but agreeable and unified disorderliness of his own making. It took a while, but eventually he no longer was a child hiding behind a book in Asheville, pushing inwardly upon himself in an effort to escape the disharmony of family, to escape an outward but unenthusiastic participation in town and neighborhood. It took a while, but eventually he opened up, in his own way, to the university world around him.

2. Bully Bernard

Of Wolfe's four freshman classes, his favorite, by all odds, was Greek, taught by William Stanly Bernard. Bernard's nickname was Bully, and so he was called by faculty, townspeople, and students, though not with impunity when in his presence. In truth, he was pugnacious, quick-tempered, sharply critical, utterly disdainful of student insouciance and ignorance, but withal a winsome teacher.

In the fall of 1916 Bully Bernard was forty-nine, a grey-haired bachelor who dressed in the latest fashion, his wing-back collar never awry, the pince-nez glasses hanging precariously from his nose, his cuffs shielding his wrists below his coat, the handsome cuff links ostentatiously visible. The cigarettes which he constantly smoked, both in and out of class, were carefully and diligently placed in a long holder, and later the butts just as carefully and diligently removed.

Bully was exacting in class. With his penetrating eyes in continuous motion, he moved rapidly about the room, pulling at his cuffs as though to cover his hands. On the blackboard he wrote Greek letters and words, beautifully formed. Always he held fast to a piece of chalk. If a student was guilty of some uncommonly stupid reply to a question, the piece of chalk was swiftly on its way in the direction of the offender.

Students loved Bully, but they naturally were a bit frightened by him, for he could be witty and cynical at the same moment.[1] "His stern charm and the fierce Sword of his tongue," Wolfe remembered.[2]

Bully Bernard was a native of eastern North Carolina. He had aspired to be an Episcopal clergyman and for several years had attended a seminary. Eventually his devotion to the ancients won out over religion. He taught here and there, received a B.A. at Chapel Hill, pursued graduate study in the North without receiving a doctorate, and returned to the campus as associate professor of Greek.[3]

His idolatry of Greek literature and culture he effectually communicated to his students. To hear him say the word *Greeks* was "a lyric experience," his voice clicking on the *G*, trilling on the *r*, undulating on the *e*'s, clicking again on the *k*, and melting softly away on the final *s*.[4]

Xenophon's *Symposium*, famous but spurious account of a conversation with Socrates, cleared the way for the chef d'oeuvres of first-year Greek: the beginning three books of the *Iliad* and Book 6 of the *Odyssey*.[5] Though Wolfe was well prepared for advanced Greek, his closely annotated and heavily marked copies of these texts, now in the library at Harvard, evince his hours of concentrated study. Bernard's plan was to top the year with selected orations of Lysias. Classes spent solely in translating from the original were interspersed with lectures on the Greeks. On the back of a letter from his brother Ben in February, 1917, Wolfe jotted down notes on Homeric Troy and Mycenae, on Schliemann and the excavation of Troy.[6] Later, he recalled an incident in Bernard's class: "Once, when I was reading Homer—I was sixteen—I asked the Greek professor if Helen was not very old when Troy was taken: it had worried me so much that I had figured it out, and knew she must be more than 50. And that old man, who had lived so long among this ageless and unwasting beauty, flayed me with his bitter tongue."[7] But even Bully's "bitter tongue" could not make the Greeks less enchanting for Wolfe. In his second year, he translated Plato's *Apology, Crito,* and *Phaedo*—a rather formidable task for a seventeen-year-old. And then came the tragedies: Aeschylus' *Prometheus Bound* and Euripides' *Alcestis.* Other Greek plays, including those by Sophocles, were read in Gilbert Murray's English translations. Bernard was prone to slight Aristophanes.

In Wolfe's day, Bully's bachelor quarters (he was later married) were at the intersection of Franklin and Raleigh streets, in a picturesque Italianate cottage, erected in antebellum times as a law office. There he kept his Twomley, an automotive vehicle the shape of a bathtub with bicycle-size wire wheels. No more than two could ride in it, the driver and one passenger just behind.[8] Wolfe called it a "pussy cart."[9] Students envied Bully his contraption, and joked that, when missing from his regular duties, he might be found in "the ditch on the Durham Road."[10] A familiar sight on Saturdays was Bully at his cottage, removing the motor entirely from the Twomley to tune and clean it. As Wolfe gradually got on more familiar terms with Bully, he was taken for rides, and it was "a comical sight" to see Wolfe "squeezed into the back with his doubled-up knees projecting above the sides."[11]

One of the reasons for Bully's popularity with students was his hearty involvement in campus affairs outside the classroom. He advised debaters, coached plays, attended literary society meetings, spoke at chapel exercises, taught Sunday school, and generally made himself available. As Wolfe strove for improvement in debating, he sought out his admired professor for instruction, but "almost invariably disagreed" with the advice given. The two would argue the points and, according to Bernard, "On the occasion of one such dissidence [Wolfe] got up and left without a word" and did not return for a long time. Wolfe "was too subjective and too emotional to make a first-rate debater," wrote an interviewer who had talked with Bernard, "even though he liked to expound and orate."[12]

In 1921 Bernard faced a situation common to many favorite professors. Under the leadership of men like President Harry Woodburn Chase and Edwin Greenlaw, chairman of the Department of English, the university was energetically attempting to discard its image as a Southern back-country college, while aspiring to bona fide university status. Professors learned that they could no longer expect promotions without publications and/or the doctorate. Bernard had neither, and when he was passed over for the full rank, he enlisted the aid of Albert Coates to collect letters from students and admirers to place in his dossier. Wolfe wrote: "I thank you for the opportunity of expressing my opinion about Mr. Bernard. I studied Greek for two years under him and I look back upon his course as one of those which have stimulated and inspired me. I think he got as much consistent work out of me as any teacher I had work under, and you know a teacher deserves some kind of wreath for his fate, who gets steady work out of me. I worked for him because Mr. Bernard is a real teacher and not an academic automation. . . . It has been two years [*sic*] since I left his class-room but I have maintained my relation to him all the time and I have been helped . . . by his advice and suggestions, just as he has helped others in their turns." Nothing would please him more, wrote Wolfe, "than to know it [his estimate of Bernard] has found favor and approval with the committee." [13] Whatever ultimate influence this letter may have had on the matter, Bernard was soon appointed to a full professorship.

Wolfe's four years' study of Greek, two at the Fitting School and two at the university, had lasting effects. From the Greek men of letters, he came to understand form, control and restraint, even if his private purposes did not always require them in his writing. He grasped the Greeks' "perception of beauty in the commonplace," their deep humanity. [14] He appropriated their glorious and unusual words (words like "phthisic"), their flowing sentences, their rhythmic style. In translating the *Phaedo*, he went to one of the sources beyond his beloved English Romantic poets.[15] The Greek legends became his everyday property. Bernard declared that Wolfe "fell for Greek."[16] And so he had, and for Bully too, who had opened up this sweeping panorama for him to look upon. "He liked Horace Williams," said a friend of Wolfe's, "but I rather think that he regarded Bully as a greater philosopher."[17]

In after years, the Greeks did not desert Wolfe, nor he them. "I can still read my Homer after a fashion and I do believe I could still put up some sort of battle with Xenophon,"[18] he wrote. On difficult occasions, he could humorously shock those present, and put an end to any heated discussion, with a stentorian rendition of lines from the *Iliad* in Greek.[19] This, of course, was Wolfe in motley. During solemn moments, though, he never forgot that "There's not much cant and twaddle to the Greeks; they are really the *living*, aren't they? The dead are all about us."[20]

3. Sophomore

In early June, Wolfe took the train from Durham, and on the way to Asheville stopped for a short visit in Winston-Salem, where his brother Ben worked for a newspaper.[1] Again at home, since any vacant rooms at the Old Kentucky Home were kept ready and available for summertime boarders, he slept at his father's house on Woodfin Street.[2] Indolence, even for an erstwhile university scholar, was not tolerated on the Wolfe premises, and the book-minded young savant was put to work. Ralph Wheaton had lately been moved from Raleigh to the Asheville office of the National Cash Register Company, and there Wolfe was given employment. "Tom is working for Ralph," W. O. wrote Ben, "it dont amount to much He only gets 5.00 a week but keeps him from loafing the streets."[3] Fred, in from Ohio with a broken arm, attempted to reestablish his former authority over his younger brother, but Wolfe announced that he'd be damned if Fred would ever boss him again. "I'm my own man," he said, "and I'm taking orders from you no longer!"[4] Following that happy and sad and confusing freshman year at Chapel Hill, he was determined to assert a new, if still somewhat restricted, independence.

A not unexpected corollary to his nascent emancipation

was a quest for women, young and old alike. In midsummer
W. O. wrote that his son had "become suddenly girl struck.
With two or three affairs lately He had better cut it out for
the present at least."[5] But Wolfe had no notion of cutting it
out. Dance lessons, started by John Terry in Chapel Hill,
continued in Asheville. Many years after, he remembered
that refulgent summer, the popular songs he hummed, the
places he went, and his infatuations: "The girl I had and
never took—Taught me to dance 'Poor Butterfly—Though
her heart was breaking' . . . The Sun Parlour—The Langren
[Hotel] roof. The dance hall and the roof garden . . . Smith's
Drug Store . . . The ecstasy of ice cream soda . . . The place at
Battery Park."[6]

And the old insistent, never subsiding hunger was there
too, the physical torment of the sixteen-year-old: "The summer's laughter—Miss 'Smith'—She had a boy aged 17—Would
not perform without some little gift—So long as she was sure
I attached some value to it—The buxom legs—The flowing
syrup—Took my medal as guarantee . . . The first night I went
up to her room. The quiet dark steps . . . Upon the bed—
Twice I performed—'You got me that time'—'I've been offered five dollars by a man right in this house!' "[7]

He visited his sister Effie Gambrell and her family in Anderson, a South Carolina town that, down from the mountains, "sweltered under the terrible sun." He remembered
"the burnt foliage, and the red clay banks," and he could
never forget "The South Carolina taste—abundance and rich
seasonings Heinz tomato sauce; Worcestershire; chow-chow;
pickles; okra soup; corn; string beans; roast, or fried Chicken;
great slabs of tomatoes; mayonnaise; succotash, candied yams;
hot biscuit; pickled peaches; apple dumpling."[8] His reputa-
tion had preceded him. He was, so the report went, "quick"
with the girls, and when he visited a young lady in the evening, the door to the adjoining room was left ajar, and there
the family kept watch.[9] Tom Wolfe was, rumor had it, a

jaunty, though considerably dissipated, university student who could not be trusted with well-bred Southern girls.

The summer of 1917 was also the summer of Clara Paul. Reflecting on the affair, Wolfe wrote Mrs. Roberts: "Did you know I fell in love when I was sixteen with a girl who was twenty-one? Yes, honestly—desperately in love. And I've never quite got over it. . . . I've forgotten what she looked like, except that her hair was corn-colored."[10] Clara Paul was from the small town of Washington in eastern North Carolina, one of five children whose deceased parents had left them well provided for. She had completed a course at the state woman's college in Greensboro and was engaged to be married in late summer to a soldier. One final vacation before the wedding seemed sensible enough, and on the recommendation of a friend, she arrived at the Old Kentucky Home accompanied by her eleven-year-old brother Ray, who was recovering from a recent illness. Some of her family disapproved of her choice of husband and hoped she would find in Asheville other interests which might turn her from marriage and allow her to develop a career in singing. Though not a pretty girl, Clara was an attractive one, with milk-white skin and undeniable freckles. At Mrs. Wolfe's she was quite the proper young lady and spoke candidly of her approaching wedding. Everyone liked her and wished to make her vacation a pleasant one. Mabel and Ralph Wheaton took Clara and Ray on a trip to Mount Mitchell, leaving Wolfe behind at Ralph's office.[11] For shorter excursions to Riverside Park and up into the mountains, Mrs. Wolfe assigned her son as escort for the two. "If Tom will go," Clara said to Mrs. Wolfe, "I'll pay his fare everywhere." Soon it was apparent that Wolfe had developed an excessive, inordinate affection for the girl. On one occasion—with Clara, Ray, Mabel, Mrs. Wolfe, and the smitten youth all present on the broad porch of the boarding house—Mabel blurted out, "Mama, did you know your baby has fallen in love?"[12] Wolfe's face reddened in embarrassment.

Meanwhile, Clara took a considerate but subdued view of the matter, and wrote her sister: "A nice young boy, here, the son of my landlady, has a crush on me. He hopes to become a writer. He has right much talent, I think. The most trivial thing he says sounds like poetry. Of course, I told him right away that I was engaged. I explained that I could never return his feeling. I was real sorry for him. But he seemed to understand. He'll get over it, I feel sure. He is little more than a child, and doesn't seem much older than our Ray."[13]

Wolfe's recollection of his love for Clara is as romantic as it is actual: "Clara—Moonlight and the holding of a hand— How her firm little breasts seem to spring forward, filled with life The festered wrist—Her tender care—Parting—The train —The letter."[14] All this may have been adolescent fervor, but the experience was a deep one, and the angst remained. Nor was it diminished when he learned that Clara had married the soldier soon after her return to Washington.

During the summer Wolfe kept alive his plan to transfer to Princeton. Now with support from Mabel, no longer in Raleigh where she could be near him, he dispatched inquiries concerning enrollment there. A formidable obstacle, of course, was his father. In mid August he wrote his freshman English professor Holly Hanford that if he went to Princeton, he supposed "poor old U. N. C. will in time manage to lift its drooping head and bear up under its loss."[15] But poor old U. N. C. was never put to the test, and whatever happened, his proposal to attend Princeton was filed away forever. Again he visited Ben in Winston-Salem on his way to Chapel Hill, and was on campus September 13 when President Graham spoke to the thousand students of their duty in wartime, a duty which, "if truly conceived and heroically done, is as important, and I dare say as difficult, as that of the men in the trenches."[16]

The university had, in truth, become a veritable military encampment. Football had been dropped. Many of Wolfe's old friends, Verne Johnson and French Toms among them, had not returned to school. A wounded Canadian army captain and two assistants were in charge. The students were divided into four companies. Reveille was at six, taps at ten. Superimposed upon his normal course load, Wolfe was required to attend five hours of military lectures a week, and spend additional long hours in close-order drill, bayonet practice, and bomb-throwing. In Battle Park he helped dig a trench—6½ feet deep and 3 feet wide, lined with protecting parapets—which was used for exercises in defense against flank attack or frontal enemy charge. As the war intensified during Wolfe's sophomore year, so did the military bustle on campus. Being much too young for active service, Wolfe participated willingly and patriotically as a member of the university Company C.[17] He was not, he regretted, among his fellows who departed the village almost daily for training camps to the north and south and west.

It was a hard time, but not a sad time. The world was not a dusty world, the days were regulated and tidy, the hours prescribed and ordained. "Our lives," wrote Wolfe, "moved to the tolling of the great bell in South building."[18]

For the first time he lived in a college dormitory. The peregrinations of his freshman year, his constant movements from rooming houses to off-campus cottage to downtown store, were over. In one of the New Dorms, so called because they had been completed as recently as 1912, he found a haven. The $10 a month was higher than the fee for space in the older buildings, but only in the New Dorms was there hot running water. In Battle #4, at the ground-floor southeast corner, he shared a suite of rooms, one for study and one for sleeping, with J. Y. Jordan, an Asheville friend, and George B. Lay of Raleigh, both several years older than Wolfe. Jordan was a talkative young man, a musician of sorts, a reader of poetry, and an active member of the Dramatic Club along with Frederick Cohn, Dougald MacMillan, Lacy Meredith, and

George's sister Elizabeth Lay.[19] In contrast, George Lay tried to take his studies seriously, thought of himself as a writer, and was an assistant editor of the *University Magazine*. Both were fond of Wolfe, and it was a happy threesome, with Lay attempting to study in spite of the noisy bull sessions carried on by Jordan, Wolfe, and any friends who casually dropped by. Convincing themselves that the crowded daylight hours on a wartime campus sapped their energies, Jordan and Wolfe poured over their books but little. One evening, to please himself and his roommates, Jordan declaimed "The Shooting of Dan McGrew" with dramatic voice and gestures. Not to be outdone, Wolfe surreptitiously grabbed the printed text, and thirty minutes later, recited the poem entire. "How did you do it?" Jordan wanted to know. Wolfe's explanation was that he "just read it through twice carefully."[20] Not always was Wolfe such a show-off, and from time to time he fell into a mood of absorption from which apparently nothing could shake him. Jordan recalled an evening when Wolfe began to undress for bed, but stopped suddenly, his eyes fixed on some object the other side of the room, and without saying a word, stared at it "with one sock removed but still in his hand" for most of an hour. He then finished undressing, his clothes scattered wherever they dropped, and climbed into bed.[21]

This was a new Wolfe, different from his freshman portrait. This was sophomore Wolfe, matured by a summer's experiences in the ways of the world, now held secure and protected within the friendship of Jordan and Lay, and ready to make his mark. Remembering the awkwardness and suffering of his first year, he decided to balance the account. Early in the term, when freshmen were still as green as the weeds growing on the banks of the Durham road, he and Bob Devereux, a graduate student, planned to go hunting cedarbirds. Though hazing had been outlawed at Chapel Hill since the death of a student in 1912, harmless infractions occurred frequently.

One mild prank, traditional on many campuses, began with inviting two freshmen to hunt cedarbirds in the nearby woods at night. Off they would go, and when deep among the trees, the freshmen were instructed to hold a sack while the upperclassmen stepped aside to drive the cedarbirds into it. After a lot of shouting, the older students crept silently back to the campus, while the freshmen, unfamiliar with the area, wandered about until dawn. Wolfe and Devereux successfully pulled off the hoax, but not so successfully that they escaped apprehension. They were summoned to appear before the Student Council, where they knew that if they were found guilty, their case would be referred to the faculty for a decision on whether to expel them from the university. The minutes of the Council for this period no longer exist, but it is recalled that Wolfe and Devereux were freed without penalty. The cedarbird incident was Wolfe's first and last brush with the Student Council.[22]

The pattern of Wolfe's classes was little changed from that of the first year. Again he had Bernard in Greek. He continued Latin with George K. G. Henry. Two Latin comedies, the *Menaechmi* of Plautus and the *Phormio* of Terence, were followed by Horace's satires and epistles, then Tacitus's historical monographs the *Agricola* and the *Germania*.[23] Wolfe's well-worn texts with their minute interlining remained in his personal library for the rest of his life.[24] His course in General Descriptive Chemistry, even under distinguished ex-president of the university Francis P. Venable, and a course titled Introduction to Psychology seem to have left no impression on him. That fall in Edwin Greenlaw's survey of English literature, he made his first A at the university. All these classes he attended obediently, with A's in English, B's in Greek and Latin, C's and a D in psychology and chemistry. At mid term in November, his report showed absence from class two times, from Chapel none.[25]

On the last Saturday evening in September, the Di Society

held another successful smoker, once more declaring its intention of becoming "a social organization as well as one
whose purpose [was] to train orators and future statesmen.
. . ."[26] At the Di Wolfe was associated with LeGette Blythe,
William H. Bobbitt, Edmund Burdick, Ben Cone, and others
who figured in the annals of his undergraduate days. In a
debate on the question of consolidating the University, the
Agricultural and Engineering College in Raleigh, and the
State Normal School in Greensboro, Wolfe won honorable
mention, but his negative side lost. During meetings, unlike
such a careful and intellectually cautious student as Clement
Eaton, Wolfe was quick-witted and lively. Once, amused by
a speaker who made little spitting sounds, he arose to a point
of order and complained: "We came here expecting an oration, but instead we are getting an expectoration."[27] And
there at the Di Wolfe again was often in the company of John
Terry, now in his senior year the assistant editor-in-chief of
the *University Magazine*.

Wolfe's hazy notion that he would like to become a writer,
even though nothing by him had ever seen print, was now
taking definite shape. The idea had been strong in his mind
when he was in Margaret Roberts's class.[28] Certainly he had,
the past summer, spoken boldly to Clara Paul of his intention.
Perhaps he had confessed his dream to Terry. In any case,
it seems that Terry pestered him to write for the *Magazine*,[29]
and Wolfe said he would try. George Lay was also on the staff
and may have prodded him.

His offering, "A Field in Flanders," its three stanzas hardly heralding the birth of a new talent, must surely have required minimal creative effort, so ardently did his blood
surge with patriotism in the autumn of 1917. Acceptance by
the editors was a foregone conclusion, and from Asheville on
November 21, W. O. wrote his son, "I will be glad to see your
poem when it appears. I dreamed something about it last
night."[30] In the delayed November issue was Wolfe's first
published writing:

The low, grey clouds are drifting 'cross the sky,
  While here and there the little smoke puffs break,
And now and then the shrapnel bursts on high,
  And growling guns their mighty thunder make.

A war-ripped field,—with what a tale to tell!
  A tale to cause the souls of kings to quake,
And here, within a smoking, bloody Hell,
  Ten million risk their lives for Freedom's sake.

And to the right a ruined village burns,
  And to the left a wood its secrets hold,
But in the gutted field the plowshare turns
  A grinning skull which sneers its message bold.[31]

The by-line read "Thomas Wolfe," but thereafter he also used T. C. Wolfe and Thomas Clayton Wolfe for his contributions to campus publications. The full name indicated his awareness of a practice favored by three-name nineteenth-century poets such as Coleridge, Shelley, Mrs. Browning, Rossetti, Emerson, Poe, Whittier, Longfellow, Holmes, and Lowell (Walt Whitman had not yet swum into his ken), and truly "A Field in Flanders" was a nineteenth-century poem written in Chapel Hill where the nineteenth century lingered softly along the paths beside the fieldstone walls. The bell in South Building may have sounded to him like the imagined church bell of a "ruined village" in France. The December issue of the magazine printed Wolfe's second poem, a tribute "To France," whose soldiers heroically persisted "When Huns came down with bloody hand, / And left fair Belgium desolate."

Though the war incessantly occupied student minds and hours, it brought little change to the village. The population was small, students and townspeople knew each other, and everyone walked everywhere. Automobiles had the taint of the *nouveaux riches*. "There are more baby-carriages in Chapel Hill than the combined number of automobiles, carriages, and wheelbarrows," noted an observer, who opined that Chapel Hill and nearby Hillsborough were "the centers of learning and history of North Carolina," Raleigh on the southeast "the center for hundreds of years of North Carolina culture," and Durham to the east "a monument to the progressiveness of North Carolina." A mile away in Carrboro, site of a railroad station, dwelt "people whom one doesn't know."[32]

Within the limits of this "idyllic spot," Wolfe came and went with confidence. After drill in early morning, he consumed "the heavy pan cakes of Swain Hall," which later felt "like lead in the stomach." The day's routine and the evening meal were sure to be followed by attendance at the Pickwick Theater, where flying peanuts filled the air and the floor was "paved with crunching shells."[33] Laughter and shouting—"Long live Annette and Theda!"[34]—drowned out the energetic playing of the performer at the piano. At eight o'clock, when the Pick let out, Wolfe trooped to the post office and was one among the "maddened, jolting mass" impatiently "waiting for the sign 'Letters Up' to be raised." Perhaps he hoped for a check from his father, but no, there were only the daily paper and a notice that the box rent was due.[35] Back on the campus, he might stop by a friend's room for a bull session and, if none was in progress, amble over to the Y.M.C.A., where he was sure to find a group of students talking and discussing the war and other weighty matters. He seemed to spend as much time at the Y as in his dormitory room, and if the "session" continued past midnight, he was known to crawl up on a couch in the reading room and sleep till morning.[36]

In discussion he "would trip along for several sentences," then hesitate, puffing at a cigarette, while searching for just the right word before proceeding.[37] His favorite expressions like "green and pink thingamabobs"[38] and "Eureka!" and his talent for clowning endeared him to his fellow students. In the *Tar Heel* of November 10, 1917, the editor inserted this filler:

"Stump" Howell (in moot court) to Tom Wolfe, who
is on the jury—"I challenge Mr. Wolfe."
Tom—"Not Guilty!"

When not in the mood for clowning, he was quiet and re-
tiring. But whatever his mood, his developing traits of personality—"some of them lovable, some grotesque, and all ex-
traordinary"[39]—brought him the popularity he consciously
sought.[40] Often he was seen "stalking across the campus,
shoulders stooped, a scowl on his face, long legs eating up the
gravel paths."[41] Did no one see him when suddenly his spirits
soared and he leaped, squealing, high into the air?[42] During
this wondrous period of his life, he wrote his mother: "I find
myself an everlasting source of interest. Sounds egotistical,
doesn't it? College life does more things for one than I would
have ever dreamed."[43]

He was neglectful of his appearance. His curly, unmanage-
able hair was seldom cut. Invariably he arrived late to class,
"wearing a borrowed shirt, coat and trousers which he had
outgrown and which were mostly worn out,"[44] a classmate
recalled. Another friend was in doubt whether or not Wolfe
was deliberately playing the role of "unwashed genius," but
stated that certainly he acted as if he were.[45] Though the story
sounds more apocryphal than actual, it is said that when
Wolfe was invited to the Dean's house for dinner, his companion pleaded with him not to go looking like *that*; but
Wolfe was unmoved and argued that "A genius doesn't have
to be immaculate."[46] There was, of course, a modicum of
truth to such a yarn. Later in the school year Wolfe reminded
Ben of a suit of clothes Ben was no longer wearing and how
he would like to have it. "I wear my uniform on drill days,"
he explained to Ben, "but Tuesday, Thursday and Saturday
afternoons we have no drill. Most of my stuff is getting frayed
except the new suit. . . ."[47] His unnecessary frugality was due
less to the unavailability of money than to his reluctance to
ask for it. "Write me," his father advised him in early autumn,

"and I will send you some spending money if you need it."[48]
Wolfe could of course depend on his father for any reasonable
sum, especially after "A Field in Flanders," but he resented
the servile dependence. He confided to his mother "the em-
barassment [sic] of writing home" for money and hoped he
soon would be allowed a bank account of his own.[49]

Wolfe's limited wardrobe and unkempt appearance did
not inhibit his social life. He spent Thanksgiving in Raleigh
visiting George Lay, whose father was rector of St. Mary's
School, a junior college for women. W. O. wrote his son that
the visit was a "fine" thing in that it would allow him to
"mingle with refined and cultured people."[50] Raleigh had
three girls' schools, and the college boys thought it high sport
to "line up in groups outside the churches where the girls
attended, and wait for them to come out. Then they would
snicker and talk among themselves, as would the girls."[51]
After the Raleigh visit Wolfe's mother inquired how many
of the girls he flirted with or made love to, then wrote, "I
hope you had good dinner on that day."

In George Lay and his several sisters, Wolfe had acquired
affectionate admirers. He was scarcely back from the Christmas holidays in Asheville when, on a Saturday evening in
early January, he attended a party for Ellen Lay, over from
Raleigh for a visit. In her diary Ellen wrote that "Tom, J. Y.,
Mr. Turlington [from whose freshman English class Wolfe
had fled], and the man in the house were there. Mr. T. and I
danced the Virginia Reel together. . . . Gosh he is good looking. . . . Lacy Meredith was also present. He and I sang 'Come,
Come, I love you truly' together. He sang sop. and I sang
bass." On "Sunday night Tom, J. Y. and George came around.
J. Y. read us the end of two slushy stories. Tom is as wild
about playing the Victrola as I am. I like the way his hair
curls in front." After her return to Raleigh, Ellen noted that,
with winter examinations just completed at the university,
"Tom and George are here. George flunked his German! . . .

unions to the general welfare, on the minimum wage law and the eight-hour day, on old-age pensions for industrial work-ers.[57] He listened with pleasure, for he was stimulated by words, charmed by the power of speech, and delighted by those rhetorical devices used in "the direct statement of ideas and emotions in language designed to persuade. . . ."[58] He and F. L. Hurley were chosen to represent the Di for the important intersociety Sophomore Debate with the Phi on the question of whether "the present policy of Government operation and control of the railroads should be made a per-manent policy." When the debate was held, Wolfe began in the accepted formal style: "Mr. President and Gentlemen of the society: No more important problem confronts the people of this nation, than the question of what policy they shall pursue with the railroads of this country. . . ."[59] The affirmative team from the Phi won over Hurley and Wolfe.[60]

For all his seriousness, Wolfe was habitually absent or late for Di meetings[61] and, when the customary 25¢ fine was im-posed, would rise to explain that his tardiness was due to "prolonged effort on his poem." Wolfe would then read what he had written, and a fellow conspirator would move to ex-cuse the fine in view of the excellence of the lines. Laughter.[62]

The March issue of the *University Magazine*, its contents exclusively patriotic, printed Wolfe's poem "The Challenge," and his first work of fiction, "A Cullenden of Virginia,"[63] short story narrating the plight of Roger Cullenden, scion of an aristocratic family noted for its bravery. During an assault in France on a German position, Cullenden, overcome by fear, decides to mutilate himself rather than participate in the advance. A chance meeting with a wounded comrade from college days obliterates his panic. He lifts the man in his arms and, under heavy fire, carries him out of danger. Cullenden is killed at the moment of safety, but happy in the realization of his courageous action. R. H. Thornton, professor of jour-nalism, commented in the *Tar Heel* that the piece resembled de Maupassant's famous story about a coward. "Many of the descriptive touches are good. The denouement might have been handled a little more effectively, perhaps. Mr. Wolfe's two contributions to this issue give promise that he is to do much excellent work in the future. He writes well and with much imaginative insight." [64]

It was not "A Cullenden of Virginia" but "The Challenge" which brought Wolfe a sudden burst of fame. Availing himself of the style and meter of Lowell's angry antislavery poem "The Present Crisis," Wolfe directed his lines defiantly "at the luckless head of Kaiser Bill." The last stanza began:

> We have taken up the gauntlet,—we will answer
> blow for blow,
> You have sent your blood and iron, pay thou then
> the cost, and go.

Wolfe originally had written: ". . . pay, thou dog, the cost, and go!" but "the more conservative element on the editorial staff felt that the words 'thou dog' were too strong—not that the Kaiser didn't deserve it, but that they jarred rudely upon the high moral elevation of the poem, and upon the literary quality of the Carolinian magazine." [65] Though Wolfe strenuously objected, Terry, for one, insisted upon the change.[66] Professor Thornton thought that the poem "perhaps sets the high water mark" for the March number, for "It is full of fire and its rhythm is well sustained. . . . The poem has many excellent lines and the dignity of true poetry." [67] Thornton's words of praise were copied in the Durham newspaper, and on April 5 the *Asheville Citizen* ran them under the headline "Ashevillian's Poem Favorably Received," reprinting the six stanzas entire.[68] W. O. wrote proudly to Wolfe of its reception "by the people of this community, *your home.*—And maney [*sic*] have been the warm congratulations your mother and myself have received for you, by such men as Dr R. F. Campbell, Col Hodges Dr Purefoy, N. A. Reynolds and men and women of such type who are among our best citizens and capable of judging. . . . When Mr Roberts saw it he threw up his hands and cheered. Then called his whole school togather [*sic*] and red [*sic*] it aloud to the entire school."[69] Wolfe's "To Rupert Brooke," in the May issue of the *Magazine*, with its lines "I wish I could express / His beauty, truth and loveliness," caused no such stir.

Back in the autumn Wolfe had written his mother how he had "entered into some outside activities for it will never do to make the text book your god."[70] Perhaps he merely planned to "enter" them. The boisterous scene in Battle #4, to say nothing of time-consuming military chores, evidently obviated his intention. But in the spring semester, daily perceiving the wasting away of Burdick, he plunged into student affairs as if life were fleeting and he no longer had time to squander. His participation in "outside activities" became frantic. "The Sophomore Year at College," he recorded in the Autobiographical Outline, "Inquiries about Clara The awakening of ambition—Begin to 'join' The awaking [*awaking* crossed through] flowering of the joining spirit."[71]

In mid-February he wrote Ben that he was going out for track and would "try to make the quarter mile. I have only one competitor and he has the advantage of having had more experience. However, I have the strides on him and if I can get away at the beginning I see no reason why I shouldn't make the team and perhaps my letter this spring. This quarter mile is a very devil of a race. It is just long enough to be tiresome and just short enough to keep you sprinting all the way."[72] Since his success or failure is not known, doubtless, as in his freshman year, he eventually gave up in disinterest. Organized sports were never to be among his college pursuits.

Though university regulations delayed membership in a social fraternity until the beginning of a student's second year, it was not until March that a tardy but welcome invitation was extended Wolfe by his friend Rupert Johnson

(Buddy) Crowell.[73] Actually only a small percentage of the young men were "taken in" by the fraternities. Social life at the university, Wolfe noted, "was badly balanced," and students who did not belong "had very few material resources to compensate them for not belonging."[74] In the Pi Kappa Phi were already a number of Wolfe's friends, and Raby Tennent had "a premonition that he [Wolfe] had the inherent qualities we aimed at,"[75] for the Pi Kappa Phi sought for members on the basis of scholarship and leadership, without regard to the social standing of their families in home communities.[76] In 1917 the chapter was only three years old, and because of its newness and its policy so different in selection from that of the old-line orders, the members of established fraternities like Delta Kappa Epsilon, Beta Theta Pi, Sigma Alpha Epsilon, and Zeta Psi—all dating from before the Civil War— looked upon the PKP's condescendingly and called them Dog Eyes.[77] Meanwhile, the Dog Eyes were signing up some of the most promising and accomplished men at the university. With the invitation in hand, and though ever reluctant to seek advice, Wolfe nevertheless called on J. Y. Jordan to get his opinion,[78] and later stalled Terry for four hours discussing the pros and cons of fraternity membership. "And," said Terry, "I knew all the time that he had already made up his mind to join."[79]

On March 25, Richard Young guided Wolfe through the initiation ceremony, held in the rear right-hand room of the small frame chapter house facing Franklin Street across from the campus.[80] Young remembered that Wolfe "looked somewhat pale. He, like most college students, didn't know what he was getting into. . . ."[81] But he endured the uncertain ordeal, and "Next morning the blossoming colors—Happiness —Shorty [Spruill], Nat [Mobley], Ralph [Pippin], Gilliam [Wilson], Buddy [Crowell], Charley [Hazlehurst], Jeff [Bynum]," Wolfe put into his notes.[82] To W. O. he wrote: "I was initiated into the Pi Kappa Phi Fraternity Monday night after taking a 12 mile march in the afternoon. It is the greatest thing I ever did and will mean much to me."[83] Throughout the spring he attended the weekly meetings and took part in the unexciting dialogues about rushing and financing.[84]

On the following Saturday he went to Winston-Salem for a visit with Ben, was among the eighteen thousand who attended the early Sunday-morning Easter service, joined up with Chapel Hill acquaintances while Ben was at work on the newspaper, and returned to the campus on Tuesday in time for the Easter Dances.[85] "The Moravian ceremonies—The food at the Greeks—Upstairs at Twin City Sentinel . . . 'Death makes all equal'—the flat gravestones."[86]

At the time of the Winston-Salem visit, the ever agreeable Ben was caught up in the flurry to get Wolfe a "dress suit" in time for the dances beginning on Wednesday. Under the aegis of the fraternity, Wolfe was preparing to make his entrance into campus society.

About this matter, so extravagantly important to the entire family, Ben wrote his mother: "Tell papa that I received his message in regards to the dress suit for Tom, and which I would have gladly arranged for here, but Tom insisted that he could get one that would do just as well and more convenient for him at Durham, as he says there are places that rent them there to the college boys in that vicinity and makes a business of this kind. He also says that he could borrow one from a friend of his at school who [sic] he knew if it become [sic] necessary. I had an old dress shirt, collar and white gloves in my trunk which I gave him to use as he would necessary [sic] need these articles in wearing a dress suit and would save him the expense of having to buy them. I notice he will soon be needing shoes as the ones he is now wearing are about gone to pieces and worn out on the bottoms, and tried to get him to get a new pair of low black shoes while here, as he would certainly need new ones in order to wear a dress suit to any advantage, but he said he would probably buy them later. I gave him one of my old suits which he wanted to wear while drilling, track training, baseball etc. to protect his present suit."[87]

The Easter Dances—one of them on Wednesday, three on Thursday, and two on Friday[88]—were well underway when, on Thursday morning, Mabel dispatched Ralph's dress suit from Asheville by parcel post, hoping it would arrive at least in time for the last dances. "When you get through with it," admonished W. O., "pack it smooth and nice and return it without dammage as Ralph has only worn it twice and cost when things were cheap 75.00." W. O. added that "before you go back to College again we will try to get one here for you. I am very sorry that you have been dissapointed [*sic*] but you should have let us know about it 2 weeks ago . . . You being so tall with . . . abnormal arms and legs it is next to impossible to get anything to near fit you without having it made to order."[89]

Wolfe went to the dances, dressed to the nines, no longer sitting enviously in the balcony with John Terry, looking down upon the glamour below. For the occasion the dance floor at Bynum Gymnasium had walls and ceiling draped in long leaf pine, with colored lights peeping from the greenery. Attached to decorative white columns were streamers of blue and white.[90] Wolfe attended unaccompanied, moving among the couples, tapping the shoulder of a young gentleman to "break in" on his partner. He was dazzled by girls, but still shy with them on merely brief acquaintance, and had no special one to invite to the dances, unlike Beany Kinlaw, who, it was facetiously reported, had so many girls coming down on his invitation that the government had granted him a special railway coach to bring in "his flock. Everybody is requested to be out at Carrboro to see them 'alight.' "[91]

Donnell Van Noppen, later a member of Wolfe's fraternity, wrote that the only time he really ever saw Wolfe "in formal clothes was during spring dances, when we were having some girls at a little party at the Fraternity House. Tom really did dress up in his best, and was, as you can well expect, the center of attraction."[92]

His initiation into Pi Kappa Phi and his presence at the Easter Dances triggered Wolfe's total involvement in campus affairs. In April he joined Sigma Upsilon, a literary fraternity at whose meetings "the University's best writers met presumably to read and criticize each other's compositions but actually to eat pickles, cheese, olives and little cakes and drink anemic punch."[93] At Wolfe's initiation, held traditionally in the local cemetery, he stood atop a gravestone and recited from Shakespeare.[94] The members of Sigma Upsilon not only wrote stories, poems, and plays, but frequently read from some favorite literary work. Wolfe's gusty reading of excerpts from Shaw's *Arms and the Man* was well received.[95] On May 3 he joined Omega Delta, its stated purpose "the promotion and stimulation of the aesthetic and intellectual side of college life."[96] Actually it limited itself to fostering the writing and production of plays. Among those active in playwriting were W. D. MacMillan, Lacy Meredith, Elizabeth Lay, Fred Cohn, and J. Y. Jordan. At a Tuesday evening meeting of Omega Delta in March, MacMillan had read "Exempted," a three-act drama written by John Terry, T. E. Rondthaler, and himself.[97]

In early May word came from Asheville of Edmund Burdick's death on the sixth. "Tom's roommate died day before yesterday of heart failure," Ellen Lay wrote in her diary. "He had such brilliant red cheeks and such terribly bright eyes, but I never thought he would die." In an English class where Wolfe and Burdick had sat together, Professor Greenlaw read aloud a paper titled "Immortality" which Burdick had written before the days of his final illness. Greenlaw's dramatic rendition and "moving commentary" fell somberly upon the ears of the death-aware young men.[98]

Wolfe was beside himself. For days he wandered distractedly about the campus, eating nothing and drinking only an occasional cup of coffee. It was apparently at this time that he found consolation in Coleridge's "poem on the West India Slave Trade,"[99] a prize-winning ode written in Greek at Cambridge when the poet was a student there, expressing the idea that weary slaves at death are transported to their native land where, now happy, they recount the horrors they endured in their former life. Wolfe went back to Battle #4, slept fitfully in a large chair in the study, and told Jordan and Lay he could no longer remain at Mrs. Abernethy's. His grooming and dress were more disordered than ever, and Lay had to remind him to bathe. After Lay left for military service, Wolfe settled in, and there he remained until the end of the term.[100] "He was like a lost soul," Jordan said.[101] Nathan Mobley remembered how Wolfe sought answers to such philosophical questions as "Why did he die? Where has he gone? Is there life after death?"[102]

One can believe, looking back on that winter and spring of 1918 from a distance in time, that Wolfe sensed what would be the ending of the Burdick drama slowly unfolding itself before him. Mortality was somehow inconceivable to him, yet it was absolute and near. And so it was that he, no more than a tall slender boy, threw himself more furiously than ever into the life available to him as if he were putting inevitability to a test.

On May 7—could the news of Burdick's death have reached him?—he was initiated into Amphoterothen, student club organized and sponsored by Professor J. G. de Roulhac Hamilton to practice extempore speaking and promote the study of good citizenship and good government.[103] Already he had been appointed as one of three associate editors of the *Yackety Yack*, college annual.[104] On May 15 he was elected to the post of permanent class poet, and two days later, he and Terry were named the two assistant editors of the *Tar Heel*.[105]

The weekly gatherings of clubs and activities filled in the terrible days. In the evenings, if there was no group to meet with, he stepped across the greensward to the University Inn

for one of "J. Y. Jordan's after supper speeches."[106] And there
were times when he slipped away to Raleigh to see "Lillian
Price, the priceless and motherly whore—'Lillian, Let me in.'
The grinning negress; the strong odor of antiseptic—The
chained blinds and the lattice work."[107] Durham was closer
by, and if he was penniless and his inner turmoil unbearable,
he borrowed $3 from a friend: 50¢ for the jitney ride to
Durham, $2 for a prostitute, and 50¢ for the ride back.[108]

The problem of money was naggingly and constantly with
him. He had not been permitted the personal bank account
he so wished for and needed. Though indulgent, W. O. had
no intention of being prodigal, and his letters to Wolfe, if
kindly and concerned, insistently questioned and reproved.
"When is your next board due" (January 29, 1918). "Be as
economical as you can" (February 1). "Enclosing small check"
(from Baltimore, February 16). "I am enclosing you check
for $40.00 which I hope will cover your present needs. be
sure to pay your board out of it first for next month and then
let me know how you stand and if it sees you through. . . .
Ralph is the owner of a Buick Car now and hope he is satis-
fied" (from Asheville, March 26). "I understand through Bens
letter that you have no shoes. If this is so let me know at once
and at what price you can buy a pair and I will send money
at once" (April 8). "I am inclosing you check for 10 00 for
the shoes. I hope however you will buy them as cheap as you
can. . . . Now I think that your college instinct would impell
[*sic*] you to write Mr Wheaton and at *least* thank him for the
use of his evening suit" (April 17). "I have just Received your
last letter and feel very proud that you have won such renown
on the Hill. You say you need $50.00 to settle up these debts.
I am inclosing you check for 75.00 pay them up at once and
if you have aneything [*sic*] left pay it on your next months
board bill" (April 23). "Pay on your bills far as this goes re-
larding [*sic*] your Spending Money for the Comencint [*sic*]
balls. At the very last of the session. let me know the Amount
it will take to get you off the Hill *clean*—and back to Asheville

and I will send check covering it and do with this 35 oo what you please . . . Take good care of Ralphs suit if injured I will have to pay for it. You have not Sent me the April Magazine yet. Take the price out of this check and mail it to me. . . . Your poem The Challenge has been coppied [*sic*] and printed in the Florida papers. A lady last week at house had the poem cut out of a Florida paper. Ben said it ran in the Winston Journal. And I find it has been coppied with your name as author More or less all over the Country. but then dont let it turn your head or make you vain. I suppose I am the one it has turned *fool*. Robt. M. Wells a university man declared Saturday Eve it was the greatest patriotic poem published since this war commenced, and would go down as such in history, and said he was going to write you at once, and that W. N. C. [Western North Carolina] Could not spare such as you, and you must Not Enlist in this war" (May 13). "I am proud of All your Achievements and honors of college. and further of all I hope you will make good use of your tallents [*sic*] in Many different Ways. Now when you return home go at once to Azalia, 5 miles East of Ashe. and try to get you a Job there are some College boys at Work there they are paying good Wages. . . . You Say you need 27 50 to leave I will Send 40 oo last of next week. As I find on May 13th I sent you 35 oo and just before that 75 oo so you cant be very hard up yet" (May 24).[109]

Early in May W. O. had written Ben about Wolfe's many college honors and commented, "All this is well enough if he behaves himself accordingly."[110] Even during this crowded and harried spring, W. O. still had hopes that his son would become a lawyer, though Wolfe had long ago discarded his father's plan. It was the winter and spring of W. O.'s second trip to Johns Hopkins Hospital[111] to cure or arrest the cancer of the prostate already beginning to destroy him. Ed Burdick was gone, and in the middle of May young American soldiers in France rushed off to Château-Thierry and died like flies.

4. Edwin Greenlaw

At the beginning of his second year in graduate school, Wolfe wrote Mrs. Roberts that she was one of "only three great teachers in my short but eventful life," though he hoped to add a fourth at Harvard.[1] The other two were Horace Williams and Edwin Almiron Greenlaw.

A native of Illinois, Greenlaw had come to Chapel Hill in 1913 after eight years as Professor of English at Adelphi College. An A.B. from Northwestern University in 1897 was followed by M.A. and Ph.D. from Harvard, where he had accepted enthusiastically the stern research methods of George Lyman Kittredge. A brief teaching assignment at the University of Chicago fired him with a "zeal for good teaching" as practiced by J. M. Manly.[2] An advocate of intense discipline with "a vast scorn for superficial thinking and sloppy work," he nevertheless communicated to his students his "dedication to learning and an infectious love of literature."[3] A pupil and later a colleague of Greenlaw's wrote that "Students and staff were fond of Ed and admired him, even though his grouchy, bearish deportment could be quite disconcerting."[4]

During his last three years at the university, Wolfe was nearly always in one or another of Greenlaw's classes. Exceptions were the short autumn quarter of 1918 and the last quarter of his senior year. The truth is that for Wolfe, ever in search of mentor and guide, Greenlaw appeared propitiously on the scene only a year after the departure of Mrs. Roberts. Yet Wolfe had reservations about Greenlaw, perhaps from the very beginning. Later, in notes for a projected play to contrast Williams and Greenlaw, Wolfe wrote amusingly that his English professor was "a strong, active man in the very prime of his life. He is a tireless worker and rarely gets to bed before three in the morning. His hero is Sir Francis Bacon and his slogan is method. He is a thorogoing, teutonized scholar and swears by the Ph.D. Recently he said to a man who protested that creative work deserved quite as much distinction as Ph.D. work: 'My dear sir. If William Shakespeare should come here and matriculate to-morrow and offer Hamlet for his doctor's thesis would we give him a degree? No. He's not a Research Man. He's like you (he told my friend with faint irony) he's a Creative Artist.' "[5]

In the autumn of 1917 Greenlaw began the year's course in English literature with Shakespeare, then went on to Bacon, Milton, Pope, Wordsworth, Shelley, Browning, and others,[6] all along proclaiming his theory that literature was a transcript of life. (Greenlaw's subsequent series of textbook anthologies for high school were titled *Literature and Life*.) Early in the semester Wolfe handed in a theme on "The Third Type of Shakespearean Humour as exemplified by Jack Falstaff" and wrote on the outside: "Professor Greenlaw, I failed to have this in class. Will you please accept it now? Thos. Wolfe." At the conclusion of the theme Wolfe playfully noted: "I can imagine this inscription on his [Falstaff's] tomb: 'Here lies Jack Falstaff—(and lies and lies and lies).' " Greenlaw admitted his student's "Lively reaction" to Falstaff, but criticized the paper for "the quite obvious superficiality of your analysis. You have not penetrated the subject —merely glossed it." The theme received a 2- [B-], as did the four pages of "A Comparative Analysis of the Characters of Richard the Third and Macbeth," handed in on October 26. Wolfe concluded that Richard's downfall was due to no one but himself, while "Others duped Macbeth and he was destroyed because of this." Greenlaw scrawled in the margin, "This is a bit too strong."[7]

To blend Shakespeare with "life," Greenlaw had a habit of baiting students with such questions as whether or not Ophelia was a nice girl: "would she object to cabbage being cooked in the home; would she drive a Packard or be content with a Model T Ford?"[8] To spark attention during the study of Milton, he passed around the Doré drawings. Wolfe remembered such esoteric bits of learning as Coleridge's distinction "between destruction and division."[9] He relished all of it, delighting himself at times in high-spirited mockery of the English writers he loved by spouting the old joke: "My Lord," said an attendant, "my lady waits without." "Without what?" "Without food and clothing." "Feed her and bring her in."[10]

In his junior year Wolfe took Greenlaw's popular English 21, a composition course based on current affairs and daily events, which met in Old East at the north end of the second floor, one of two class areas in a building with twenty-eight dormitory rooms. "The ceiling is patched in some places," wrote a student, "and needs patching in others. The benches show the effects of time and of many knives. The heating and lighting are uncertain."[11] In this cheerless space, Greenlaw experimented with *writing* and "life." He urged students to hold a "point of detachment,"[12] at the same time warning them he would pass no assignment having in it those abhorred expressions: "in our midst" and "along these lines." Among Wolfe's classmates were LeGette Blythe, Jonathan Daniels, Paul Green, and John Terry.[13]

Invariably Wolfe was late to arrive. He had overslept, of course, then dressed hurriedly, while scribbling his assignment on bits of paper, and hastened to class without pencil and textbook, without breakfast, and even without part of his clothing, but always with his homework crumbled in his pockets.[14] Meanwhile, the students has assembled, and Greenlaw was on his rostrum. "Well, let's get on, gentlemen," the professor would say. "Last time we were—" At this moment a clatter of heavy footsteps from "the old wooden, winding stairway; the door bursts open; Tom's head appears and he looks around cautiously before making a dash to his seat. E. G. has stopped cold. For a full minute he says nothing; then, sardonically: 'Brother Wolfe, we welcome you. Will you read the burning words you have written for us?' Tom shuffles to the front of the class. He slips his big hand in one well-filled pocket after another. His air of distress increases until at last he feels into the inside coat pocket: with a sigh of relief he begins to unfold" his written assignment "and reads for ten minutes at a fast clip, rewinds the sprawling manuscript, glances with twinkling eye at poker-faced Greenlaw, and sits down."[15] According to a fellow student, Wolfe would scrawl a few notes as he got ready for class, then hold "the class, as well as Dr. Greenlaw, practically spellbound during the whole period from his few moments of reflection while dressing."[16] On days when Wolfe was not scheduled to read a paper, his tardiness was nevertheless tumultuous, and Greenlaw would wait till Wolfe was settled before resuming the lesson with the comment: "Now that the thunder has passed. . . ."[17]

The most fondly remembered yarn of Wolfe's shenanigans in Greenlaw's class is the episode of the toilet paper. There are many versions, but the story generally goes like this. The assignment was a theme on "Who I Am." As usual, Wolfe was late, stood in the doorway with Greenlaw's suspicious eyes upon him, then took the cylinder of paper from behind his back and rolled it in on the floor, explaining it was all he could find the night before. The students roared, but Greenlaw quieted them and told Wolfe to begin reading. After some twelve paragraphs, Greenlaw interrupted him. "Mr. Wolfe, I'm going to make only one comment on your theme. All I can say is, by God, it's written on the right kind of paper."[18] LeGette Blythe insists that of course Wolfe had plenty of theme paper at hand, and that it was all merely another of his carefully planned acts to get a laugh, relying on Greenlaw's forbearance.[19] On other days, Wolfe would pull a scrap of paper from one pocket, read from it and complete the sentence from another scrap of paper in another pocket, sometimes finishing with words written on a matchbook.[20] Wolfe's tomfoolery was fast becoming one of the more pleasant aspects of campus life.

Early in the winter of Wolfe's junior year, Greenlaw organized the class into a Peace Conference, with groups of students representing delegations from important nations. Issues were investigated, and "after due discussion and debate each question at issue was settled by a vote of the Conference."[21] Germany was demilitarized, amounts of reparations specified, territories adjusted, new countries like Czechoslovakia and Armenia set up, and a Constitution of the League of States adopted. Luther H. Hodges represented Great Britain; Moses Rountree, France; Ben Cone, Belgium; Nathan Mobley, Russia; and so on. Wolfe was one of the five representatives of the United States; he headed the Commission of Indemnities, and was a member of the Commission on Freedom of the Seas. Though the twelve-week project was prolonged by sharp contention on many points, the *Tar Heel* reported that the class wished to finish its work "before the constitution drawn up by the Peace Conference in Paris was made public," and added that Greenlaw was "pleased with the work of this group, which he regards as excellent training for thoroughness in research and exposition and speed and intelligence in debating."[22]

Wolfe was in his glory. No longer late to class, he along with the other students eagerly waited outside Old East for

Greenlaw "until he came up the walk of mornings," greeting them "Brother Mobley," "Brother Wolfe," "Brother Spaugh."[23] Wolfe's pockets were filled with jotting he had made since the last session. In one of his formal speeches, he declaimed, "Mr. Chairman: Yesterday, after that eventful session, I was approached by one of the members of the Russian delegation, Count I Dontnowhosky, and reproached for refusing to allow myself to be dominated by pure principle—for proposing, in fine, a compromise between Principle and Expediency. But, Mr. President . . . we must not allow ourselves to forget the great American people who we represent—a people who must have more than highly abstract phrases. . . . Please do not conceive our ideas as of the maudlin, sentimental, Bolshevist variety—it is a dream now—but we hope to make it possible by building on a rock. . . . And, as the American people are a nation of dreamers who dream from facts, we will fashion our league according to the demands of the immediate present and let Time bring about the evolution."[24]

On completion of the Peace Treaty, Greenlaw invited the class to his home to celebrate. Hilton West's write-up of the party was so breezy that Greenlaw thought Wolfe was the author.[25] "Ze Grand Finale du Chapel Hill Peace Conference," ran the account, "convened Monday evening dans le palais du M. Greenlaw . . . beautifully situated just on the outskirts of the metropolis—the Seine winds below it almost circling the royal grounds. . . . Col. Slinklinelski Wolfe . . . arose in all his Americanism. He told of the interesting career of Count Forrestus Miles-schof, chairman of the Balkan delegation before being elected secretary of the conference, he spoke of the important reports of 'all present' and the still more important motions [*sic*] 'let's adjourn' that Count Mileschof had made. . . . Dr. Greenlaw then invited the guests into the adjoining room where a vision such as only seen in the golden age of Greece, a table laden with the fruits of the gods met their gaze. Surely Peace had been restored to earth. The

German supped at the same board with the Frenchman. . . .
With rousing yells for Dr. and Mrs. Greenlaw the peace conference adjourned for the last time, one of the greatest classes
ever held within the historic walls of U. N. C."[26]

The Treaty was printed, many copies were sold on the
campus, the *New York Times* suggested editorially that it
was probably about as good as anything which might come
out of Versailles, and the New York Public Library ordered
a copy for its collection.[27] The humor section of the university
yearbook, in its fabricated account of a day's work at the
Peace Conference, has Wolfe, "unfolding by degrees his seven
feet two of framework," address the conference: ". . . I sug-
gest that we settle the much disgusted question of 'Freedom
of the Seas' as follows: Build a chute-der-chute from the top
of the Eiffel Tower into the Atlantic Ocean. Let it be greased
with Swift's Premium Brand Lard, and made staunch and
stout by heavy timbers. At some appointed date, say July 1,
let the Kaiser be carried to the top of the tower, placed in a
small boat which there awaits him, and at the hour of twelve
meridian let the strand that restrains the small boat be sev-
ered. I ask you, Gentlemen, could you come to any more
satisfactory sol-yution of this many-sided question of 'Freedom of the Seas'?"[28] The yearbook writer had faithfully ap-
proximated Wolfe's current humorous style.

So triumphant was the Treaty project that Greenlaw immediately planned a similar one on the American city, with
groups of students representing laborers, businessmen, poli-
ticians, reformers, and anarchists. An episode was forecast in
which labor would go on strike in certain industries,[29] and in
preparation Greenlaw read John Galsworthy's play *Strife* to
the class. "How his grim mouth loved it," Wolfe remembered.[30] As the days passed, the project was altered to the
writing of a collaborative problem novel centering on a clash
between capital and labor, throughout which would run a
story of "absorbing human interest."[31] With the term nearing

an end, progress was slow. A few students contributed, but the bulk of the work was turned in by Wolfe,[32] whose chapters had to do with "the breaking of the strike and the two men on the verandah high above town Greenlaw said I had achieved 'style'—What most men don't get till forty."[33] Wolfe's excitement in the writing of fiction was such that he began turning over in his mind "the possibilities for a college novel" from the point of view of an "unappreciated student, because all students, no matter how prominent or successful, *felt* unappreciated."[34]

As with the Peace Treaty, Greenlaw encouraged print and exposure, determined that his students not be allowed to blush unseen. The *Range Finder*, English 21 journal of which no copy has been found, contained student views "growing out of war,"[35] and it was probably in connection with this publication that Wolfe noted enigmatically: " 'Out out Damned Spot! But No, Alas! 'Tis Waterman's' Got a I on course for it."[36]

In his senior year (once more to move ahead momentarily in Wolfe chronology) he took Greenlaw's famous course in nondramatic Elizabethan literature, with emphasis on Spenser in the fall quarter, and Bacon in the winter. He remembered "The triple allegory of the Faery Queen [*sic*]—Keats had of Faery 'Tank.' "[37] And as a mutual fondness developed between the two, Greenlaw would make a statement in class, then turn to his favorite student: "Now, Mr. Wolfe, expatiate and elucidate the matter."[38] It was during this period that Greenlaw found himself the target of student disgruntlement. So heavily involved was he in preparing his authoritative Variorum Spenser that he somewhat neglected his class. A group of students called on him with the request that they be allowed to substitute for his class a course in the modern novel, and though his vanity was hurt, he provided them with the course. Wolfe stuck with his mentor, who thereafter reinstituted the old magic.[39]

A few years after leaving Chapel Hill, Wolfe wrote to Greenlaw: "I shall always put an enduring value on your friendship. You were always a big person; you are one of the best teachers in the world. . . ."[40] When Greenlaw expressed a high opinion of his first novel, Wolfe was jubilant and quickly responded: "When you said there was 'not a shoddy line in my book' I was . . . exultant. . . . You are one of the few people I have ever known that I take literally, because what you say is worth taking literally and because as a man and a teacher there was never an ounce or a grain of shoddy in you. . . ."[41] Wolfe wished to remind Greenlaw "that the men who waken us and light a fire in us when we are eighteen are so few and rare that their image is branded into our hearts forever. . . ." It was Greenlaw "the Grim Ironist," Wolfe wrote, who was "one of the great creative forces of my life."[42]

5. Junior

Upon his arrival in Asheville from Chapel Hill, Wolfe did not seek the summer job at Azalia his father had written him about, for he had made up his mind, the day of independence at hand, to set out for Norfolk to find work in a wartime installation. Ben gave him money and persuaded the family to let him go, assuring them that Fred was stationed in the Navy there and would look after him.[1] So off he went, lured by "The fair promises of wealth in Norfolk— . . . I set off for Norfolk—The wait at Danville Richmond in the morning—Newport News—Ride across the sparkling bay Electricity of the war."[2] Four days later and almost out of funds, he ferried Hampton Roads to Langley Field, where workers were given food and "housed upon the field at company expense,"[3] and there he found a job as a time-checker, riding around the field on a horse to record the work hours of the labor gangs. Some school friends were also employed there. When a month was up on July 4 and his first pay of $80 was in his wallet, he quit the job. To his mother he wrote that it "was valuable experience" in spite of the mosquitoes and bedbugs, that he had a good suntan, and that "My boss out there told me I could have a job any time I came back." On several occasions while at Langley Field, he took the ferry to Portsmouth, where

Clara Paul, now married, was living; he stood a distance from the house but made no move to see her.[4]

Feeling prosperous, Wolfe and his friends spent a "week of riotous living"[5] in Norfolk and at the beaches, and again were soon out of money. Finally in desperation they looked up Fred at the Naval Base. They were "actually famished," Fred told Mabel, reporting that the first thing he did was to rush them to the galley for food. Undoubtedly in a Chapel Hill spirit of comic exaggeration, they bragged to Fred that all they'd had "was a can of beans a day apiece and a loaf of bread split between them."[6] And yes, they'd had a pie too, purchased for a dime found in a pocket lining. When news of the sorry state of affairs reached Asheville, Mrs. Wolfe wept for her starving boy, but Ben shouted, "Cut out crying. He's all right now. Fred's taking care of him."[7]

The next move by Wolfe and one of his friends was to make inquiries at the Government Employment Agency. They were advised to purchase carpenter tools and then, they were told, jobs could easily be found. After spending their remaining money on tools, they reported for work on Monday morning July 7, but were fired after the first day when the employer at Porter Brothers, in the process of building a quartermaster terminal, discovered they were unskilled as carpenters. The tools were sold, and they signed up at a Newport News pier, where troops and ammunition were being loaded.[8] The hot summer ground away, and Wolfe remembered the $7 he won in a crap game and the "waiting queue and the heat" at the whorehouse.[9] Finally in September, exhausted but triumphant, he took the train to Richmond—"The girl at Hayler's"—then home—"Home—Ben—The sleeping porch room—His bitterness had reached a peak—'Good God, I wonder what I'm living for.' Had been rejected for service because of lungs. 'Get all you can from them' Bitterness and humiliation—Mrs. [Annie] Trimm."[10]

During the summer and fall of 1918, the war permeated

the lives of everyone everywhere. The university officially opened on September 26, later than usual, at which time President Graham welcomed the eleven hundred students at the "Armory," formerly Memorial Hall. The quarter system had supplanted the familiar semester plan, the study of German had been abolished from the curriculum, there were vegetable gardens behind Peabody Hall, and only an improvised football season was permitted. The university had been converted into a unit of the Student Army Training Corps, dormitories were labeled Barracks A, B, C, D, and the dining hall in the old University Inn was a Post Exchange where "non-S.A.T.C. men [were] given advantage of the cut rate prices."[11] A lieutenant colonel, a captain, an adjutant, and ten lieutenants ruled the community.[12] More officers were coming. Student cadets policed the village and the college grounds when they were not drilling or studying mathematics, topography, and surveying.[13]

To his distress Wolfe's age kept him out of the Student Corps and he was placed in the "University Battalion,"[14] a catch-all for those rejected by the S.A.T.C. The non-S.A.T.C. students meanwhile followed the daily schedule, rising at six (which must have been a lamentable burden to Wolfe, even in wartime) and bedding down on the sound of the bugle at ten.[15]

At the Pickard Hotel, a three-story structure built of hard pine and painted white, and next door to his fraternity house, he shared a room with J. L. (Nip) Poston, medical student from Statesville.[16] Wolfe and Poston's dark attic room had a gabled window overlooking Franklin Street. Operated by M. William Uzzell and his wife Lula, the Pickard accommodated both transients and students. In the parlor, on the left as one entered, was a piano and also card tables at which poker and other games were played, and there before and after meals students gathered. Always Wolfe was in the center, entertaining everyone present and joining in the commotion. In the

big dining room at the back, "drummers" and students gorged
themselves on hardy meals. Designated tables were set aside
for members of any fraternity wishing one. It is remembered
that Wolfe failed to pay his last bill at the Pickard—$25 a
month for room and three meals—probably because he had
lost the sum at poker.[17]

He likely intended to pay it, but by now Wolfe was a free-
wheeling fellow not confined to the Pickard Hotel or to con-
ventional responsibilities. Often, after squandering away the
evening conferring with Forrest G. Miles, editor-in-chief of
the *Tar Heel,* he would fall asleep in Miles's room and stay
the night. Finally, Miles and his roommate Robert W. Madry,
like Jordan and Lay the spring before, put in an extra bed
for him. According to Miles, "Tom slobbered and in his sleep
would make peculiar noises as one swallowing with great
difficulty. He would grind his teeth and snore, but with it all
would sleep soundly and late." Miles and Madry delighted
in Wolfe and affectionately forgave him his bruxism and
other peculiarities. "He smoked cigarettes," according to
Miles, "and in smoking gave the impression of literally eating
them. His two fingers and the cigarette they held would all
enter the mouth at the same time."[18]

His class work was light. Besides Military Training and
two courses under Frederick H. Koch, who had just arrived
at the university to teach drama and playwriting, he sweated
through a five-hour course in General Physics under Dean
Andrew Henry Patterson. The first question on a "Make-up
Quiz" dated November 26 had to do with vectors, and Wolfe,
though sadly out of his domain, wrote out a precise answer to
it and to the other questions.[19] "Professor Patterson and the
hobby for lightning," he remembered.[20] In the winter quarter, with Military Training no longer obligatory, he continued physics, pulling from a C up to a surprising B, and the
two classes with Koch, then added Greenlaw's Advanced Composition and a first philosophy course under Horace Williams

—a program which, except for physics, he continued into the spring quarter.[21] Frequently professors entering the class-rooms discovered Tall Tom Wolfe eating on the sly from a paper bag.[22] There had been no time for a meal; he had many things to do.

Beginning in the autumn of 1918 he became happily in-volved, for the rest of his undergraduate days, in the *Tar Heel*. On the masthead of October 2 he and Terry were listed as the assistant editors. A week later he was managing editor, succeeding Robert W. Madry, who had accepted a position with the university. In November, when Forrest G. Miles left for Marine training, Wolfe's name moved to the top of the masthead, still as managing editor. During Miles's ab-sence, Wolfe wrote the editorials and most of the copy,[23] for he could no more function as "part of any organization" than he could "organize himself."[24] In his new job he speedily put on a campaign to increase the newspaper staff, often suddenly reduced when students left for military service,[25] and was a daily visitor in the dormitory room of John H. Kerr, Jr., and A. L. Purrington, two of his associate editors. At Board con-ferences on the second floor of the Y, he was always late and "tended to drag the meetings out interminably."[26]

On Miles's reassumption of the editor's job in January, Wolfe was his right-hand man. "After being up practically all night," Miles wrote, "Tom would catch the early bus out to Durham and invariably would telephone me later in the day [from the printer's] that he needed copy; whereupon, I would get together as much as I could and light out for Durham, spending an hour or so with him at Seeman's place, finishing in time for us to get a late supper in Durham and to have an evening together. He would usually know several interesting girls who appeared to enjoy our company—even though we were broke: not a cent to spend even for the movies. . . . We would return together to the Hill late at night—perhaps on the last [unscheduled] jitney (it required about an hour and a half to make the trip—never less than an hour; sometimes the roads were impassable.)"[27]

In the fall issues a penchant for humor began to be noticeable in the *Tar Heel*, surely an innovation brought on by Wolfe, who undoubtedly wrote the series called "Fables of Sultan Peikh A Bou."[28] In "Fable No. 1: Some People Get Away with Murder," Dr. C. Astor Oile, druggist "in the small college town of Maple Hill," conspires not only to dilute milk shakes but raise the price to 15¢. "No. 2: The Apparition That Walketh by Daylight" mused on the changes brought by the war, the "Drug Stores desolate and streets deserted! Ah, the piteous sound of the jitneys rattling emptily Durhamwards which were wont to whiz by jammed with joyous humanity." In "The Fable of the Benevolent Druggist and Thirsty Student," Dr. C. Astor Oile finds a young man at the threshold of his drug store. "As you love me, fair sir," gasps the student, "please part my lips and wet my parched throat with some of that wondrous elixir bedight coca cola," but alas! the youth has only "a single jit" (a nickel), the drink is a dime, and the druggist never allows himself to clear less than 300 per cent on a sale. Later, when the spring dances came around, Dr. C. Astor Oile was advertising "Tiz, Blue-Jay and other pedal remedies. Come early (before the dance) and avoid the crush."[29] Other Wolfean humor appeared in "Just Gossip," satirizing the S.A.T.C.[30]

In mid-October, the devastating influenza epidemic at its height, Ben became seriously ill, and Wolfe was called to Asheville. Ben died on October 19. "The trip home—Asleep in the Pullman That morning . . . The gripping of my wrists 'Why have you come home? Why have you come home?' The smothering death and the rising hatred in me at the ugliness pain, and horror of it all—'Oh, yes—it *is* the kind of death *you'll* have'—Their smothering presence—Papa hoisted up the stairs—Horrible pity and fury against Mama—How finally when his eyes were closed she joined herself to him and held on, and could not be pulled away . . . 'Drowning' said Colby with the yellow teeth and the big cigar, 'in his own secretions' . . . The darkness that bent the house inwards—the enormous darkness—And later—A light swings over the hill; a star shines over the town; that Earth below is very clear. I shall go down —No one but God and Mrs. Trimm (hiccoughing slightly) Wreathes [sic] from several somewhat elderly ladies for him —The hot coffee and the crowing of a cock—drugged deep in death at midnight—embalmers fluid and my enormous height Take a great deal to fill me up—The artistic undertaker and his excusable pride—The funeral preparations—A good job— A drop of beaded embalming liquid like white wax at left nostril—The rigidity . . . Mama's obsession with small worth- less things . . . Ben had it not at all. Always his own money spent it as he pleased—The cuff links he bought for me one Christmas—Found him in bed Christmas morning—Warm with gratitude for it . . . The unreality of death to anyone near you. Something which happened to old people and strangers —That this bright and particular flesh should be mortified, made one, compressed with the earth be tied uniquely—But even then I did not believe that I might die Before twenty you are young and you can never die—Mr Brownell and the suave condolences—An undertaker's sympathy—Dr. Camp- bell and the long Scotch head." [31]

Wolfe's father was dying too, not the quick death, but the slow one. "The impending doom . . . Like watchers were we on a city wall, but the enemy comes behind. Who will be next?" [32]

After the funeral, Wolfe returned to Chapel Hill by way of Winston-Salem "to clear up Bens effects. The Zinzendorf hotel—The rising of hot lust again. So soon after passion the woman who came late at night to the room. Forbade me to put on light—the tight close passion of our embrace. By the light as she went saw that she was a negress." [33]

A rainy day back in Chapel Hill, as Wolfe and Terry were

leaving Swain Hall, "We got about a hundred feet from the Hall and stopped under an oak tree," said Terry. "Tom stood there and recounted to me the whole story of his brother's death. He told about his mother, and he used a phrase about his mother that I have always remembered. He said she sat there 'as though she were carved of marble.' "[34] Mrs. Wolfe had repeatedly claimed that there was something special between Ben and his younger brother that she could never explain. "Ben could manage him all right when he was a baby only a year or more old. . . . Ben was very gentle" and "took so much pride in dressing him up."[35] The relationship, needless to say, was the strongest of Wolfe's young life, and it was "Coleridge on Philosophy and Pain and the Fear of Death"[36] to which he turned in his grief.

Exactly a week after Ben's death, President Edward K. Graham died of influenza in Chapel Hill. "The Graham hysteria . . . A bit of the prig . . . Large spiritual eyes—the slightly beautified face—Frank, his brother, much much worse."[37] The loss of President Graham, so idolized by most of the students, left the campus in a despondent mood, and for days it was as though an ominous cloud had settled over university and village. The university, it was said, would never recover from the blow.[38] Marvin H. Stacy took over as acting president, but he too was dead three months later at the age of forty-one. Edmund Burdick . . . the soldiers in France . . . Ben . . . Graham . . . Stacy. As best he could, Wolfe dammed inside himself the suffering and terror.

With a fierce loyalty, he plunged into rescuing the declining Di Society, its membership considerably depleted. He seconded Clement Eaton's motion asking the Di faculty members how to conduct business in view of S.A.T.C. disruptions. He was elected to the post of First Corrector (one who decided if a debate was up to standard). He moved for a resolution on the death of President Graham, was of course appointed to a committee to draft the resolution, but failed to call the group together. He made speeches at the Di on university publications, on the necessity of keeping students in college. But often he was fined for being late or absent, for allowing the fines to accumulate or become overdue, and for being guilty of "non-performance of duty," as in the matter of the Graham resolution. Although Wolfe accepted responsibility willingly, his reliability was uncertain. He and Luther H. Hodges pled for a woman representative on the Editorial Board of the *Yackety Yack*, but John Terry and William H. Bobbitt were against it, and the motion was defeated.[39] Later, he was on the winning negative side of a debate concerning whether communism was better than a mandatory system for "undeveloped territories." He argued for more lively meetings of the Di, urging that freshman be allowed to "take part in the general debates."[40]

At a Society smoker, when entertainment and humor were the order of the day, "The great tragedian Thomas Wolfe arose and held the hall spellbound by the masterful rendition of a tragic oration," wrote a member. "An otherwise perfect presentation was slightly marred by the fact that Mr. Wolfe was compelled to refer to his manuscript *once* or *twice*, but this was excusable as he could, perhaps, have done better with more preparation."[41] The smoker concluded with a feast of sandwiches, ambrosia, punch, apples, oranges, bananas, cake, and ice cream. Wolfe enjoyed such gaiety but was nevertheless quite serious about his public speaking, and was chosen that year, along with William H. Bobbitt, John Wesley Foster, and Luther H. Hodges, as a featured Di debater.[42] Of more importance to the well-being of the Di than his activities at meetings or the visible comic role he played were his behind-the-scene maneuvers to sustain the organization in crisis.

A few weeks after Ben's death, the certainty that the war would soon be over left Wolfe hopelessly depressed. As with other students like him, he felt "no joy," but "tricked and cheated" that it was all ending "before we had the chance to see it." He wrote that, at the time of the false armistice four days before the real one, "I was in the South building in the room of a friend who was enlisted." Yells came from the campus below them, and an exuberant young fellow burst into the room and shouted out that Germany had surrendered. "For a moment my friend sat perfectly still. Then he uttered a single unprintable word in a tone of the most choking fury and exasperation, rose from his cot, deliberately hurled his hat upon the floor, and jumped on it with both feet." Though students responded dutifully to words like *truth*, *humanity*, and *civilization*, "What we felt," Wolfe wrote, "was that the war was glorious and magnificent, and that it offered us a thousand chances for glory, adventure, and joy."[43]

Within a month the S.A.T.C. was demobilized, and in the ten days before Christmas vacation, class elections were held and dormant university organizations reactivated. The quarter ended on December 20. Wolfe spent the holidays on Spruce Street—"the year of Ben's death—'We'll all try to be cheerful' That was a *good* Christmas."[44]

Again in Chapel Hill, Wolfe and six other returning members of Pi Kappa Phi gathered up their house furniture and moved to a new location on Fraternity Row. They settled in on Wednesday, January 7, 1919, initiated three new men in the evening, had the customary "feed," and retired. Two hours after midnight, a fire started in the Sigma Alpha Epsilon house next door, quickly spread east to the Pi Kappa Phi, then on to the Sigma Nu. With the ringing of the bell atop South Building, students appeared from every direction, salvaging what they could. For a while it looked as if the fire would jump the pathway between the Sigma Nu and the university library and set it ablaze.[45] Though the three fraternity houses were gutted, most of the furniture was saved, and the next day Wolfe and the "brothers" returned to their former chapter house on Franklin Street.[46]

With the end of the war and the S.A.T.C., university enrollment in January dropped to a mere 814.[47] Business establishments along Franklin Street, depending entirely on the patronage of students and townspeople, held on, trusting in better days to come. C. S. Pendergraft and S. J. Brockwell ran jitneys to Durham, four over and four back each day. Andrews Cash Store advertised in the *Tar Heel*, as did Foister's for picture-framing and Kodaks, and the Chapel Hill Hardware Company for razors and pocket knives. The A. A. Kluttz Company called itself "The University Book Store" with "Everything for the Student," and adjoining Kluttz's was *The Barber Shop*. A "pressing club" was operated by "Long Bill" Jones, whose charge was $1.50 a month for pressing and repairing. W. B. Sorrell sold watches, repaired them, and fitted glasses. Eubanks Drug Store was still a favorite student hangout. Dr. William Lynn had his dentist's office over Peoples Bank. "Hey, Fellows," hallooed the Pickwick Theater, "Look Who is Coming! Charlie Chaplin and Mary Pickford"[48]—as if the students didn't know. Large illustrated advertisements in the *Tar Heel* proclaimed the delights of "Murad, the Turkish Cigarette." On the campus, typewriters were "for sale and for rent" by J. E. Crayton, Jr., in 11 Old East Building; the University Book Exchange was at the Y.M.C.A.; and Swain Hall served three meals a day for $13.50 a month.

As Wolfe walked the short length of Franklin Street and ambled along the paths of the college grounds, he observed members of the faculty and their families: "First families Harvard—the Darling Boy—'Tommy' Wilson and the little Wilsons—the Dope-Drinking Dad—Mrs. Wilson nee Pickens [Pickard] and the social life of the town—Mrs. Doctor Lawford [Lawson] and the poison pen—MacNider the Great—Venable the Bitter—Gentle Toy—Joseph Hyde Pratt and the almost fatal boils—the skittish wife Mrs. Winston and the departed Mrs. James—Bitterness of the faculty life." He took note of what went on "in the barber shops—the barbers and their hound dogs."[49] He was fascinated by the story of Uncle

Andy, an ancient black janitor at the medical school, one of whose jobs was to fish cadavers from the vats of formaldehyde and cart them to the dissection classroom. Wolfe had been told how one day Uncle Andy pulled his own law-breaking son from the vat, the white burns of the electric chair on his arms and legs, and how, hoisting an old hymn at the top of his voice, he wheeled the body up to where the students were waiting.[50]

Wolfe was now six feet three inches, and still growing. Archibald Henderson, professor of mathematics, remembered his "diminutive head and pale, set face across which whirled shy, fleeting timidities, now setting into stone-gray, Sphinx-like fixities of expression, now glaring with aquiline defiance out of demoniac eyes, [and the way Wolfe] always clutched frantically and in vain at something mysterious elusive, ineffable."[51] In his junior year Wolfe was thin-chested, his viscid hands continually tugging at his unruly hair grown long to hide an exzema blemish.[52] Almost always in coat and tie, he presented a neat appearance despite the sometime careless condition of his wardrobe, particularly the "frayed crotch seams" of his trousers—"Let the cloth be doubled here. I always wore it out at this point. With the Ancients things went better—A Rabelaisian cod-piece."[53] He was aware of the "lengthening size" of his body—"but not yet painful—For on the Hill men had grown used to it—to me—A common friendliness—The growing saps still running in my limbs—Sense of elastic extension and incredible power—Longer [longing] for greater weight—But feeling of range and speed."[54]

He was hardly a scarecrow, yet the sight of him did indeed make one fleetingly aware of nature's comic incongruities. But Wolfe made the best of it, no longer hiding in a secret room above a drugstore. For the most part he transformed those stone-gray fixities of expression into broad smiles and strode forth into the center of things. Buttressed as he was by a "keen and scintillant wit," wrote Professor Koch, "his talk was shot through with a pyrotechnic exuberance which hypnotized his youthful audiences,"[55] and soon he was "in demand for banquet occasions as an after-dinner speaker."[56] More and more he projected the image of a "polite and responsive creature" with a "contagious grin and a shy-knowing twinkle in his eye."[57] His celebrity was becoming university-wide, and, said LeGette Blythe, "if you ever saw a little knot on the campus and went up there and heard a bunch of boys laughing, and you go up there, push into the middle, Tom would be in the middle telling some big lie or laughing." Wolfe had a perceptible lisp in his speech,[58] but there were deep undertones which allowed his voice to be dramatic when he chose.[59] "Doing my two inches of growth a year," Wolfe wrote in the Autobiographical Outline—"When my voice changes—not noticeably comic, but I could do with it what I would at will."[60] While talking, he would roll out a few words quickly, then swallow "with his Adams'-apple dancing up and down like an elevator on the loose," and proceed with another half dozen words.[61] It was delightful, all of it.

An anecdote, presumably concocted, has Wolfe telling how he would knock at the doorway of a house and inquire if Miss Strange lived there. "No," would come the expected answer. Turning to leave, he would mutter audibly, "Well, that's strange."[62] On another occasion he would knock and ask, "Is this the door?" before backing away.[63] A yarn he liked to repeat had to do with a testimonial he said was used in advertisements of "Tan-Bark," a patent medicine: "Before taking 'Tan-Bark,' " a lady reported, "I could not sleep with my husband, but since taking one bottle I can now sleep with any man."[64] He had a story about a mountaineer who put croton oil in some whiskey which he and a friend drank: "Both ran home; but the oil arrived first."[65]

Whenever possible Wolfe attended performances of vaude-ville in Durham, relishing the wisecracks of the comedians. Back on campus, he imposed his own style so ingeniously on the jokes that his friends thought them Wolfe's creations.[66] He flavored his speech with favorite expressions like "than which there is no whicher,"[67] and was hungry for slogans, as were most of the students in those days. John Terry tells of how his lanky friend came racing by the Library, waving aloft a copy of the *Tar Heel* and shouting, "John, I've got the new slogan—Youth Will Fix the World."[68]

But not always was Wolfe jokesmith and phrase-maker, and some of his more perceptive friends sensed that beneath the humor, the put-on, and the high spirits ran a strong undercurrent of questioning and anxiety and loneliness. Scarcely a half year had passed since that elegiac October day, and though "Ben's death stayed remote—Appeared to fade," he wrote, "from time to time" it returned "to abort and damn the moment."[69]

Frequently he was enigmatic and exasperating. One midday he invited a friend to have lunch with him "at the old Chapel Hill landmark, Gooch's Cafe, and, after ordering a sumptuous meal for both of us," recalled E. Earle Rives, "he suddenly ceased talking, picked up the menu sheet and started scribbling on it. Just as our dinner arrived, he jumped to his feet and shouted one of his favorite words, 'Eureka,' and, with the menu sheet brandished in his hand, he dashed out of the restaurant, leaving his meal untouched and the bill for me to pay." Rives accepted the fact that Wolfe was not like other students, and he was not in the least offended.[70]

Despite moments of eccentricity like this, Wolfe was eager to be a regular fellow, and in his resolute search for popularity, toward which his comic nature contributed, he was unselfish in responding affirmatively to whatever requests were made of him. That he was the first one thought of when a rally or smoker was planned was due to the certainty that he would bring humor and zest to the affair.[71] At initiation ceremonies conducted by the clubs and various fraternities, he was spokesman and leader, and, recalled a younger student,

"With his flow of words he made the ceremony for us neo-phytes entering into the Greek world a most realistic and memorable occasion."[72] Elizabeth Lay declared that in his third year at Chapel Hill, Wolfe, for all intents and purposes, "was simply running the University" and, insofar as she could tell, he always seemed to be "a very happy person,"[73] Happy he was, at least most the time, with an increasing feeling of superiority to average students, though still somewhat ill at ease in the presence of those from wealthier homes[74] or those from families solidly identified, in his mind by reason of their ancestry and prominence, with the mythical North Carolina social establishment.

Within the routine of this pocket-size campus world, Wolfe was an egalitarian prince, moving with the currents. After morning classes, he was by 12:45 at Swain Hall, dining on beans and dodging the air-borne biscuits, at the library or Emerson Field in the afternoon, at the evening meal and then at the dance floor in Bynum Gymnasium (other men students the only week-time partners available), or at the Pickwick Theater pandemonium, or at the Y, where hymn books cracked heads down front. Finally, following perhaps a modicum of study, came the best part of the day: the bull sessions.[75]

At a bull session Wolfe was king not prince. In a friend's crowded dormitory room he would launch into matters of ethics and idealism and religion, and he could pour out, to the delectation of the younger boys, enough information about women, the most constant of all topics, to last through the night—as the bull sessions frequently did.[76] When Wolfe got the floor—and did he ever fail to do so?—he would "get on a line" and drift bit by bit into exaggeration, as later with real-life situations.[77] After an hour or two of this, when the open-mouthed but study-minded students eventually were able to muster enough strength and courage to halt the quasi-soliloquy and turn him out of the room, Wolfe felt no rejection but moved determinedly in the direction of Franklin

Street, there continuing his monologue to the astonishment of anyone who would listen, whether itinerant idlers, homeless blacks, jitney drivers, or the nocturnal habitués of Gooch's Cafe.[78] On those rare occasions when he had a deadline to meet for the *Tar Heel*, he repaired to a hideaway at the Y, and there he was alone.[79]

Of this time in his life Wolfe left a wondrously confessional, if fragmentary, account: " 'Democracy' at the university —On the necessity of speaking to Everyone—How studious was I of popularity—In this junior year my gregariousness reached its highest peak—I joined everything . . . Even then, in this year of joining—my isolation was. Periods of content with different boys, a brief adventure or two to-gether,—but never a complete unfolding—with older men—partly with Horace Williams . . . A false and happy year—Enlarged opinions of our greatness—'The Big Men'—and the feeling of the greatness and importance of all around us—the School, the State, the People . . . The huge pretense of idiot geniality . . . The Creative instinct and the ebullience of the goal in me— How I ran leaping high in air with [my] teeth tearing at the tender leaves. Fuimus Fumus."[80] He left cameo portraits of some of his classmates: "Bill Bobbitt—the little man with the deep voice 'What are the issues?' . . . Jeff [Bynum], the complete moralist—the Fine Young Man—'Shorty' Spruill and the clear blue eyes—The vacant depths of purity." He left, in the Outline, a brief disclosure of his fantasies and desires: "To be celebrated and to be loved—This what I wanted at 18—Is this not what we always want . . . Delight of a tall lad in a long bed on a rainy morning, when the rain falls in microscopic particles—On sleeping a cool night through with a tender virgin—When you are 25 and she is 18—This the proper age —not 19 and 18 or 20 and 18. . . ."[81]

That Wolfe, so occupied with university affairs great and small, had time for bull sessions and daydreams is somewhat incredible. In this year of joining, he added the Satyrs to his trophy belt. Initiated the same time as Wolfe into this "elective society," composed of those who had exhibited "distinguished dramatic ability," were Jonathan Daniels and George Denny.[82] Among the faculty members were Bernard, Greenlaw, and Koch. Wolfe was active in the other dramatic group, Omega Delta, where Bernard, Greenlaw, Hanford, Koch, Norman Foerster, and Archibald Henderson might turn up for meetings to discuss serious thespian concerns with students like Wolfe, Jeff Bynum, and Albert Coates. At meetings of Amphoterothen, public-speaking honorary society, Wolfe was in touch with Coates, Clement Eaton, and T. E. Rondthaler.[83] The Y.M.C.A. put him in charge of campaigns for the "Financial Department."[84] To the twenty-five students gathered for a meeting of the Buncombe County Club, he spoke "of the many advantages which might be taken of the various college activities" and helped annihilate "a large group of cakes, candies, and fruit."[85] At Sigma Upsilon, the literary group whose faculty members included Bernard, Foerster, Greenlaw, and Henderson, it was nothing unusual for Wolfe to crash into the meeting room "a half hour late and out of breath from bounding up the stairs and immediately take charge of whatever momentous discussion was under way."[86] At initiations he was noted for whacking the backside of neophytes with powerful and painful strokes.[87]

When the *Magazine* was revived in April, 1919, with T. E. Rondthaler as editor, Wolfe and LeGette Blythe were listed among his assistants. Wolfe's "The Drammer," a 2½-page light-verse mockery of the old-fashioned play featuring villain and put-upon heroine, appeared in the first issue. "The Drammer" was a far cry, as were his poems in the two remaining issues, from the patriotic lines written for the *Magazine* when he was a sophomore. In May came "In Appreciation" by "Thomas Clayton," a spurt of humor on the Japanese longing to be at home in cherry-blossom time. "Russian Folk Song," the June selection also by "Thomas Clayton," held up to ridicule the Communist "plutocrat" who "did his daily work," but was hanged by the Reds because he was considered "dangerous to the common weal." Though Wolfe's folk tragedy "Payment Deferred" was also in the June issue, humor was now, no mistake about it, his intent, his sword, his strength.

One must pause in the rush, as he seems never to have done, to observe Tall Tom Wolfe in this Chapel Hill springtime after the war. There he comes down the steps of Old East from Greenlaw's class, where he has just been arguing the terms of a Peace Treaty. He leaps across the greensward to Proff Koch's playwriting class in the Library, there to think out the plot lines of a one-act tragedy he is planning to write. And then the best session of all: back across the grass to philosophy with Horace Williams in Alumni Hall, where his mind swirls with abstract concepts that come and go and come again to explode into bright magic.

Not all his evenings were devoted to bull sessions in students' rooms and talk, talk, talk in Gooch's Cafe. In late February he listened to Hamlin Garland lecture on present-day literature so "base and degrading" and pondered Garland's plea that "future University journalists . . . exert every effort to counteract this modern tendency."[88] Koch told his playwriting class of Garland's having "referred to an unusually serious member of his audience," and wanted to know if perhaps it was one of his playwriting students. Wolfe spoke up, saying he must have been the one, for "I'm the serious type, you know." There was hearty laughter, as there always was at one of Wolfe's mild witticisms.[89]

One might pause again in the rush to look closely at a ten-day stretch in mid-March. On Friday and Saturday, March 14–15, Wolfe acted his own hero's role in "The Return of Buck Gavin" on the first bill of the Carolina Playmakers, thereby acquiring the nickname Buck. Quarter examinations began the following Thursday. On the evening of Monday,

March 24, the last day of examinations, Wolfe was at Green-law's home enjoying himself at a party to celebrate the completion of the Peace Treaty.

In early April he doubtless attended Bully Bernard's public reading of *Enoch Arden* to a musical setting by Richard Strauss,[90] and of course he was at the Junior Class Banquet a week later,[91] when after speeches by Bernard, Greenlaw, and Williams, the great tragedian of recent fame by the name of Buck Wolf was lifted to a table in Swain Hall and, by popular demand, acted out "The Return of Buck Gavin," but this time making "the play an excruciating burlesque, using the exact words that he had uttered seriously on the Carolina Playmaker stage." Faculty and students "gathered around the table and he and they screamed with laughter as he made his play seem utterly ridiculous." The play dealt with an outlaw who lost his freedom by returning to put some flowers on the grave of a friend who had just been hanged. "The effect was about the same as when *East Lynne* is made into a farce," remembered Terry, who added, "I have seen other instances where Tom turned the mood of his writing from high seriousness to sheer comic playfulness."[92]

Shortly thereafter, Wolfe was at work on the committee to plan Stunt Night, highlight of Junior Week in late April, and may have had a hand in organizing the other events: an oratorical contest, a "Tug-of-War," tennis matches, a potato race, fireworks, baseball games, a "band concert and singing around the well," a wheelbarrow race, a lawn party, and dances.[93] On Stunt Night he warned the audience that if the actors articulated a stage direction such as "A year elapses between Sc. I and Sc. II," it was "to understand this means *us*—not *you*. You do not have to wait a year."[94] He then was one of the five actors in the Junior skit presented "under the auspices of the famous Carolina Haymakers Association, a thrilling one-act melodrama entitled 'The Last of the Nabiscos, or Why Uneeda Biscuit.' " During an interval in the program it was announced that Wolfe had been named to Golden Fleece, highest honor at the University. This was the crowning glory, but Wolfe's ego was not so inflated that he did not participate in the Junior Week baseball game between students and the all-star faculty, who won 10–9 over the Fighting Freaks led by "the great Freak twirler—Wolfe," noted for his "blinding speed and wicked benders." It was observed how, "with a cold, contemptuous sneer distorting the classic beauty of his countenance, he fed 'em over, and the desperate profs whiffed wildly at the soft Spring atmosphere." The *Tar Heel* write-up sounds suspiciously like the prose of the Freak Twirler himself.[95]

It was of that soft season that Wolfe remembered "Frank Graham and the Greensboro game—The warm opulence of the Spring—and the dances . . . 'Memphis Blues'—The man who fell backwards down the Gymnasium steps . . . Reeking corn [liquor] on everybody's hip—The circle of white damned faces looking over at the gym The almost intolerable snobbism."[96]

Meanwhile, at the fraternity house, Wolfe's routine was so unconventional and irregular that no one student felt he could "put up" with him for long. Fred Moore, one of those who "alternated having him for a roommate," explained that it was "not that he was disliked, but because his personal habits were not the best. I think this was because his mind was occupied with his literary activities rather than his personal cleanliness and appearance. In other words, he would forget to take a bath or have his clothes cleaned until reminded by some of us to do so. We often said that Tom belonged to all the clubs on campus except the pressing club, as the dry cleaners were known in those days. This and the fact that he was out to some meeting almost every night and invariably came in very late did not make him a good roommate."[97]

Wolfe's love of practical jokes sometimes backfired. One

evening the study-conscious fellows at the fraternity house rigged up his iron bed so that it would fall at the slightest pressure. Wolfe came in late, threw open the windows, undressed, extinguished the light, and knelt beside the bed to say his prayers. In the middle of some sanctimonious utterance, down came the bed, the noise of it accompanied by loud profane yells.[98] In came the guffawing jokesters, with Wolfe soon laughing too. At other times, he would barge into a group of several students conversing about a course which he had not taken, capriciously grab an opposing point of view, and demolish their theses and arguments.[99] Perhaps to entertain his listeners he might recite some lines from Shakespeare or a bit of nonsense he had heard. Gilliam Wilson recalled one of his favorites:

> "Old man, give us a story."
> The old man rose and thus began:
> > "The wind it blew
> > And the snow it snew,
> > And the lightning flashed
> > On the mountain top."[100]

Wolfe was the Grapter (historian) of his fraternity, in whose journal he wrote that a banquet to honor the alumni was planned for the Yarborough Hotel in Raleigh on April 5. His successor reported the dinner was a great success.[101]

The fraternity house was setting for an irksome short period in that spring season of Wolfe's glory. Expecting with some certainty their election to Golden Fleece, pinnacle of university accolades, Wolfe and Nathan Mobley were told they must be in their rooms every night at nine o'clock, the hour when, they had been informed, the "tappers" *might* arrive. Though confinement was contrary to Wolfe's customary meanderings, he dared not be absent in case the "tappers" came. The men in the house "took advantage of the situation, cloaked themselves in sheets, and submitted him to initiation ceremonies of their own creation." When he discovered the fraud, he of course "fumed at length over this maltreatment."[102] Two weeks afterwards, the real "tappers" appeared, blindfolded him and Mobley, and in an initiation which lasted until dawn, led them blindfolded "through the woods and fields and across the streams of Orange County in a ritual representing the voyage of Jason and the Argonauts in search of the Golden Fleece, during which paddles were freely applied."[103] Not until Stunt Night was the election of Wolfe and Mobley, of Luther H. Hodges and "Shorty" Spruill and three others, made public.[104] These seven students, it was generally agreed, were the "most representative men" at the university. "The growing fame—Golden Fleece —The mock initiation and the real one,"[105] Wolfe recalled. And though one might expect a boy of eighteen to have his head turned by the honor, such was not the case, for Wolfe always looked forward to the next achievement, never back to the last.[106]

At the end of May, in the contests for various campus positions the following year, Wolfe was unopposed for the editorship of the *Tar Heel*.[107] In the winter and spring quarters, as his titles multiplied, so did his grades improve. Two A's came from Greenlaw, two others from Koch and Williams in the spring. There were no C's, then or thereafter.[108]

The final acclaim of his junior year was announced at Commencement in June, when he was awarded the Worth Prize in Philosophy for "the best thesis submitted" by a student in Horace William's class. Wolfe's prize essay, *The Crisis in Industry*, argued that, with the war over, labor had "come into a realization of its self [sic] as a body vital with the power of life, intelligent as to its workings, and sure of its function in industry." Labor deplored capital's incapacity to understand this new image, and if strikes and "class warfare" were to be avoided, capital must recognize labor's right to self-determination and assist in the creation of an "industrial democracy,—a system of democratic co-operation in industry with equal rights and responsibilities for labor and capital."[109] No longer would labor be patient in subservience. *The Crisis in Industry*, so different from former Worth Prize winners, was hardly a maximum effort for Wolfe, who at the Di Society had time and time again heard long-winded debates on labor unions and labor disputes. As a matter of fact, in its "lecture-platform style,"[110] the essay read rather like a Di Society declamation. But no matter, for it was rumored that, whatever the competition, Horace Williams, lone contest judge, had already decided that the prize would go to "the most brilliant student I ever had."[111] Two hundred copies of the fourteen-page booklet were printed.[112]

That Wolfe's father rejoiced at these extravagant distinctions, there can be no doubt, but the old man's illness seems to have blunted his pen, and if communications of any sort came from the dusty world of Asheville, busy Thomas Wolfe no longer stashed them away.

6. Proff Koch

In 1918 when Frederick Henry Koch came to the university at Greenlaw's invitation, he had already established himself as a successful composition instructor in the field of folk drama. A native of Kentucky, he grew up in Illinois, attended Ohio Wesleyan, and after a teaching stint at the University of North Dakota at Grand Forks, obtained a master's degree from Harvard, where he sat spellbound in the drama classes of George Pierce Baker. Following his return to Grand Forks, the staging under his direction of plays by Lady Gregory and other Irish dramatists led him to encourage students to write and produce comparable plays of the American folk. From the beginning, their little one-acters were enthusiastically received, and in 1917 the undergraduate playwrights and actors were christened the Dakota Playmakers. Though Koch was happy in his work and had no wish to desert his burgeoning enterprise, a milder climate was needed for his wife and two young sons.[1] Then fifty years old, Proff, as he insisted on being called (and be sure to spell it with a double-*f*!), was a dapper figure always dressed in a tweed Norfolk jacket and Windsor tie.

In spite of the S.A.T.C.-dominated university in the fall of 1918, Koch arrived at a propitious time, the climate ripe for folk plays. For several years the Dramatic Club had staged works by Shakespeare, Pinero, and Shaw. Two clubs, Omega Delta and the Satyrs, encouraged campus drama. Dialect and folk yarns made their way into the *Magazine,* where stilted sentimentality was progressively giving way to local color, as in "The Sea Is a-Cryin'," short story of fisherfolk in the October 1917 issue. Earlier, freshman Paul Green and G. W. Wimberly, associate editor of the *Tar Heel,* collaborated on "Old Cronies," produced by the Dramatic Club, one author "playing the role of an old student and the other that of a sea captain."[2] For production during the Community Spring Festival in May, Professor Hanford in charge, Green and Harris Copenhaver had original plays ready.[3]

Before the opening of the fall quarter in September, Koch had been provided a classroom in the Library, and there he set up what he considered an atmosphere for playwriting, with playbills and photographs on the walls, the bookcases filled with volumes of dramas. Around a large table, with him at the head, would sit the students in an aura of informality, friendliness, and creativeness. When the students finally arrived—more than a third of the two dozen co-eds and a lone male, Wolfe—the ever-optimistic Koch was momentarily bewildered. "Proff," Wolfe reassured him, "I don't want you to think that this Ladies Aid Society represents Carolina. We have a lot of he-men seriously interested in writing here, but they're all disguised in uniforms now. I tried to get myself into one myself but they didn't have one to fit me!"[4]

Koch began by talking of the folk drama, its history and importance. He spoke of North Dakota and his work there. Wolfe reported that he confessed to the class a week later, "I can't tell you how to write a play. There's only one real way. Go ahead and write it. . . . And starting is the hardest part. I can only advise you now to draw up a synopsis of your plot and your story and wade right in. Go on through to the end without stopping, if possible. Then go back, condense, expand, revise as much as is necessary. Then bring it before the class and read it." But what was folk drama? the students wanted to know, since Koch assigned no textbook. It was a play "written from characters known in person to the author and from scenes familiar to the writer's own experience,"[5] a play of the *people* coming from the soil. *Listen, my students,* Koch might have said, *look homeward, and there you will find your play.* In the folk drama, he believed, lay the "regeneration of the degenerate modern stage."[6] This class would be a beginning, and the movement would spread out through the state.[7] To get the "movement" underway, Koch admonished his students to delay no longer, for he promised that as soon as he received the first scripts, they would be read before the class and a round-table discussion would follow. Eventually there would be an authors' public reading, and a vote by ballot for three plays to be staged.

Here was the man for Wolfe, the man with the "One Idea," the "Man with one obsession," the man possessed with "Fanatical zeal."[8] Wolfe, swayed for a while by his admiration of George Bernard Shaw and fired by Koch's fervor but neglecting his advice, started his "modest career as a 'play-maker' by attempting a satiric comedy. It was a false start. It was a dismal failure," he wrote.[9] Not yet had he learned that, instead of imitating the British refinement of Shaw, he would need to employ words like *belly-taut, mush,* and *spindle-shanked,*[10] locutions like *that air* and *hit ain't.*[11]

Besides playwriting, Wolfe took Koch's courses in Shakespeare and the early English dramatists. Though Koch was no scholar, he knew the field well, looking upon the plays as vehicles for actors, not as documents for academic scrutiny. During the class hour, as he strode back and forth reading the precious works, he changed his voice dramatically to portray the different characters. Yet Koch was no "crip" teacher, for he required students to keep vocabulary sheets and copious notes,[12] and his examinations were comprehensive, like the one in December, 1918, when he asked questions on Lyly, Greene, Peele, Marlowe, as well as on Shakespeare. A third of the examination concerned "The Folk." He wanted to know about farce in the mystery plays, about the manner in which "the folk instinct manifests itself in the Robin Hood and the Mummers' plays."[13]

Meanwhile, shamed by the failure of his Shavian comedy and unsuccessful in his search for a more suitable subject, Wolfe conferred with the always resourceful Proff, who pulled from his folder of Play Ideas a clipping with a Chicago date line saved from the *Grand Forks Herald* of June 10, 1906. "To Place Flowers on Pal's Grave—Outlaw Lavin Seeks to Honor His Comrade and Is Nabbed by Police" ran the headline above the story:

> Five weeks ago Charles Coleman laid down his life for his friend, Patrick Lavin. On the dreary plains of Texas, with the loot of a bank in their saddle-bags and a sheriff's posse close at their heels, Coleman turned his cayuse in its tracks, drew his pistols and for a moment stood off the officers of the law.
>
> His body was riddled with a hundred bullets—but in the darkness Lavin made his escape. Coleman died laughing in the face of death and of Sheriff Searborough, of Lee county. Today Lavin was arrested in the Chicago home of his sister.
>
> On the table at his side reposed a huge bouquet of lilies of the valley. His black sombrero lay close by, his clothes were carefully brushed. He was just about to visit Rosemount cemetery and place on the grave of Coleman a last token of his undying friendship.
>
> The door of the room in which he was standing swung and Lavin looked up quickly into the barrels of the revolvers in the hands of Detectives Conick and Culvane. Instinctively his hand went to the left breast of his coat,

where hung a Colt's 44, but before his fingers would close around the stock the officers had the upper hand. Lavin dropped his hands to his sides.

"All right, boys," he said. "You've got me, but I wish you had been half an hour later. I wouldn't have cared then, because I would have had these daisies [*sic*] on Charley's grave and you could have arrested and be —."

Lavin is known in Texas as "Cyclone Pat." He is a gun hold-up man, a safe blower and an enemy of society. He was a bad man, but Sheriff Searborough knew him.

When Lavin disappeared into the darkness of the Texas night, and the officers knew that it was useless to follow further, the sheriff hurried to Chicago to look out for Coleman's funeral for the other bandit.

Lavin was unavoidably detained. He was living in the desert, and could not get to Chicago in time for the funeral. Today he reached town. He went to the home of his sister, sent for the finest flowers that money could buy and was ready to start for the cemetery when arrested.

"Oh, I don't care what you do with me now," he said to the officer. "The game is not worth playing without a pal, and nobody looks like Charley to me. Send for the sheriff and take me back. I don't care," he added quickly.

"I wish," he added quietly, "you would pay a kid to put those flowers on his grave, though."

And a boy was paid, and the flowers today mark the resting place of "Cyclone Pat's" pal.

Wolfe read the clipping. It was "a far cry from the mountains of Western Carolina," he thought. "But when the dramatic possibilities of this incident flashed upon me, I immediately started to work with a set of mountain characters, the principal being Buck Gavin, a mountain outlaw."[14] The play he wrote was no less melodramatic than the Chicago news story. Buck's dying friend Jim Preas, during a gun battle with the sheriff and his deputies, urges him to escape. Returning to his mountain cabin, Buck dispatches his sister Mary to pick some violets (Playwright Wolfe's favorite flower)[15] to take to Jim's grave at "the top o' big Smoky," and while she is absent, meditates on how the revenuers "allus git" the moonshiners. The sheriff enters silently, a revolver in his hand, soon followed by Mary "with a large bunch of violets." Buck's parting words as he calmly goes away with the sheriff are "I would've liked to 've took 'em up there, an' . . . an' . . . sort o' looked 'round. But . . . well, I reckon I cain't go now . . . but ol' Jim'll know . . . jes' the same. Sis,—you take 'em."

Whether Wolfe wrote "The Return of Buck Gavin,"[16] as he said, "at one sitting, on a rainy October afternoon"[17]—the October of Ben's illness and death—or whether he scribbled it off in the early morning hours before he was scheduled to read it in class[18]—is immaterial, for it was a *gen-u-wine* Proff-style folk play and Koch had no way to know nor would he really have cared that, though Wolfe was intimately familiar with boarding houses and a university campus, "characters known in person to the author" did not include a sheriff and a moonshiner.[19] The streets of Asheville and the docks of Norfolk were "scenes familiar to the writer's own experience," but not "the top o' big Smoky" or a mountain cabin. With unreasoned confidence, Koch was pleased when "The Return of Buck Gavin," along with Minnie Sparrow's "What Will Barbara Say?" and Elizabeth Lay's "When Witches Ride," was chosen for his first bill.

In no small or modest way did Proff Koch promote his students, himself, and his One Idea. Before his students' work was presented to public view, the drums must beat and the trumpets sound. "The ethical practical—Would convince himself that any labor he was engaged in, of whatever sort, was sanctified," Wolfe noted years later. "Idea of service—and passion for advertisement—of self first of all."[20]

Proff laid the groundwork. Announcement of an organizational meeting of the Carolina Playmakers, a "community movement," was made in December. Townspeople, the faculty members and their wives, were to become actors and make-up artists. He sought further exposure a few days later by reading Dickens's *A Christmas Carol* to an enthralled audience of students and villagers in Gerrard Hall.[21] In January he lectured to all and sundry on "Playmakers and the People," prophesying the creation of "a new poetry democratic—a fresh art-expression of the folk, rich and strange, and of enduring beauty."[22] The *Tar Heel* editorialized that "Success is not a thing to be hoped for by the Carolina Playmakers. It is assured."[23] On the last Friday in February, Koch, "assisted by Mrs. P. H. Winston at the piano," read *A Midsummer Night's Dream* to "a crowded house and attentive audience."[24] He subjected himself to undergraduate savagery by agreeing to be initiated into drama-supporting Omega Delta.[25] Though Wolfe knew he was a favorite of Koch, he was never obsequious. At the initiation, Koch was blindfolded and made to bend over at ninety degrees for paddling, "though he—and we—thought it was only a gesture as far as he was concerned," remembered LeGette Blythe, who was present. "But not Tom. When we laid those paddles on the student initiates, Tom gave Proff a healthy swat or two on his pants-tight backside, and Proff came up erect and, I always thought, with his professional dignity as well as his anatomy ruffled and stinging."[26] Anything to advance the One Idea!

Attracting the most promising students to his playwriting class was a necessary aspect of Koch's promotional campaign. In January, when the campus overflowed with war-returned veterans, Koch edged into a group of them at registration to talk about his course. In his belted Norfolk jacket "with bulging big pockets," he was an appealing figure.[27] Wolfe, too, did his share of proselyting. One of Wolfe's converts was Moses Rountree, who recalled how, in the classroom, "Wolfe sat two seats from me, his loose frame overflowing the chair, his elbows propped on the table as if to support his towering bulk. He looked like some half-civilized half-man. . . . His dark hair was tousled and wild. . . . His sensuous mouth was curled at the corners in an amused half-smile." He looked "like a serio-comic bumpkin," wrote Rountree, and nobody "in the class took him seriously—Tom saw to that. He was constantly making wisecracks and inviting joshing at his expense."[28]

During February Koch was indefatigable in planning his first bill of one-act plays. An "adjustable stage" was set up in the auditorium of the Chapel Hill High School. Among those on committees were professors Bernard, Greenlaw, Henderson, Thornton, and even Wolfe's freshman mathematics teacher, John W. Lasley, plus an assortment of village ladies. At try-outs, when no one could be found to play the lead in Wolfe's play, Koch told him: "I guess you'll have to play it yourself, Tom. You may not know it, but you really wrote that part for yourself!" "But I can't act, Proff. I've never acted." "You're a born actor," Koch assured him, "and you *are* Buck Gavin."[29] Since Koch was directing another play, rehearsals for "The Return of Buck Gavin" were conducted by Bernard.[30] Mrs. Alga E. Leavitt, a faculty wife who was playing the role of the old hag in "When Witches Ride," pitched in to tutor Wolfe in acting.[31] Leila Nance Moffatt was Mary, and Wolfe's friend Frederick J. Cohn the sheriff.[32]

Among the capacity audience for opening night, March 14, were scores of students who were unconcerned about dramatics, but who dared not miss an exploit by popular Tom Wolfe.[33] To introduce the plays, Greenlaw spoke of the Carolina Playmakers and their "conscious deliberate attempt to translate North Carolina life, with its rich store of tradition and romance and varied and interesting human types, into dramatic form." This night, he predicted, was "a night which will prove historic."[34]

For his appearance as a mountain outlaw, Wolfe borrowed Nathan Mobley's sweater to pad his thin shoulders.[35] On cue, Buck Gavin entered the mountain cabin—the "towering, angular form," the stride formidable, the movements deliberate.[36] And at the end of the play there he stood—the heavy-hearted outlaw "with a ridiculous little bunch of violets in one hand."[37] The audience had sat in rapt silence; no laughter had greeted the tragic lines by an erstwhile favorite campus comedian Buck Wolfe.[38]

If certainly no masterwork, "The Return of Buck Gavin" was even so a commendable effort for an eighteen-year-old. Backstage afterwards, when his affectionate mentor Bully Bernard offered some critical comment in the spirit of helpfulness, Wolfe glared at him, "his eyes flashing, his long body hunched over, and his mouth open at the remarks of the director. He stood indignant for a moment and then wept his mortification."[39] Yet truthfully, Wolfe was not altogether pleased with the play. "Someday, anyway, I'll write something worthwhile," he said.[40] "A rainy day and *The Return of Buck Gavin*—A folk play? Then what is *The Importance of Being Earnest?*—The day of Buck Gavin— . . . Bully Bernard."[41]

The popular local success of "Buck Gavin" prompted Wolfe to the writing of another play similar to it. In "The Convict's Theory"[42] a lawbreaker returns to the mountains from the penitentiary to kill his doublecrossing brother. The uncompleted manuscript, showing meticulous changes from *there* to *thar* and *it's* to *hit's*, generated "Deferred Payment," a one-act play appearing in the June *Magazine*. In this second version the returning convict Jack discovers his girl Lucy married to his traitorous brother Sam, and during the bitter confrontation, Lucy takes the revolver from Sam, who is then stabbed by Jack with a knife and dies muttering, "He will pay!"

While the dating of Wolfe's manuscript plays and drama fragments is precarious at best, there are occasional clues.

"The Strikers,"[43] its setting the home of a mill worker in a small North Carolina town, obviously came from Wolfe's study of industrial conflicts in Greenlaw's class. The hero, a strike leader, valiantly holds out for a 20% increase in wages, but his men are discouraged and worn out, the women ill and suffering, and the strike is settled in spite of the leader, who is then fired from his job. At the time of Greenlaw's project, Wolfe was also writing his prize essay *The Crisis in Industry*. An untitled play,[44] dating perhaps from this period, concerns a well-to-do farmer who has an irrational hatred of his black laborers. When his wife discovers that he has one-eighth Negro blood, the arrogant octoroon yells at her: "I'm seven-eighths white, I tell you." A fragment, unrelated to the other drama manuscripts, narrates the return of a doctor to his American medical fraternity house from England, where he has been knighted and now is called Sir William.[45]

Wolfe explored the son-family relationship in another group. A fragment, presumably an early one, centers on an ambitious boy and his father, who is unwilling to advance the money for his son's college education.[46] In "The Family," Wolfe created an awkward dramatic situation in which a mother defends her son, just out of jail for fighting the police, against the father's anger at the boy's gambling.[47] Wolfe's initial struggle with his much-revised *The Mountains* continues the father-son confrontation. In a first, tentative version, Richard Travers, back from college, tells his father that he will not take up the family feud, that he will not "kill someone with whom I have no quarrel." As the outraged father orders him to leave the house, a mountain man rushes in to report a renewal of the feud: ". . . git yo gun an' come quick, fer Hell's a-poppin tonite. Them dam McLungs got Jim Judson this mornin' an' hits on agin. Hit'll shore be hell this time."[48]

"Concerning Honest Bob," printed in the *Magazine* in May, 1920, satirizes campus politics, a subject which, if Koch's ideal of "familiarity" was strictly to be aspired to, Wolfe certainly knew whereof he wrote. Bob, feigning innocence and honesty, humbly agrees to run for class president, knowing full well that a "campus machine" is to support him. This and the father-son group were doubtless written in Wolfe's senior year.

Meanwhile, the enthusiasm for original poems and stories and plays by students seemed to Wolfe a bright emanation within the context of the institution's "swift, new progress." In "The Creative Movement in Writing," a paper read at the final gathering of the student body on June 6, 1919, he puffed Greenlaw and Koch with undergraduate excitement and delight. He said that campus writing, so deplored in the past, was much better now that students were depending on their own experiences. The Carolina Playmakers in their depiction of "the folk lore and life traditions of North Carolina," had produced the "most distinctive work," and favorable recognition had already "appeared in two New York dailies." The Peace Treaty had been critically approved in the New York press, "the Nation, the New Republic, the Survey," and other journals. Greenlaw's students had "this past quarter devoted their efforts to the production of a novel dealing with the labor problem in a typical American community. Excellent work," said Wolfe, "has been done in completing two books of this three-book novel." For those like himself, "It may not be our lot, in our lives here at Carolina, to take part in the more spectacular activities of our college life, in athletics. But if we are not naturally endowed with athletic requirements, if we may not go out on the football field and cover ourselves with mud and glory,—remember: They also serve who only sit and write."[49]

In the autumn Wolfe was back in Proff's playwriting class where the competition of Paul Green, just then returned from the war, would have cowed anyone less self-confident than Wolfe. But the two usually got along well enough together. Green's clear portrait of Wolfe in Proff's class merely substantiates the earlier portraits by other classmates: "His procrastination usually kept him in hot water. He would wait until the night before he was to read a play, then sit up until daybreak dashing off page after page of dialogue scrawl that only he could decipher. Then he would come to class hollow-eyed, shaggy-headed, unkempt and stuttering, and babble through the reading of his play. And always there was enough in the piece for Proff and the rest of us to praise—enough of vital and warm dialogue and streaks of rich characterization tangled in with his weird and high-faluting melodrama and rhetoric to mark his talent." [50]

The second and last of Wolfe's plays staged by the Carolina Playmakers was "The Third Night," [51] given on December 12, 1919, with the author in the role of "a degenerate Southern gentleman." Wolfe wrote it, as usual, just before it was due. He retreated to Frederick J. Cohn's room in the Koch home, sat at Cohn's desk, and worked through the dark hours till he had completed it. [52] When it was produced, Cohn, Jonathan Daniels, Chester Burton, and Wolfe made up the cast. A static play less successful than "Buck Gavin," "The Third Night" is a free adaptation of Lord Dunsany's *A Night at the Inn*. [53] The time is 1858, the scene a "dilapidated dwelling" thirty-five miles west of Asheville. On a stormy evening, the third after the "degenerate Southern gentleman" had robbed and killed the father of the girl he had not been allowed to marry, the ghost of the Old Man appears and leads him away to destruction. The dialect, the setting, the supernatural element—all were qualities encouraged in Proff's folk gospel, but Wolfe was not deceived, even then. In the summer of 1919 he confessed that his plays were "but the amateurish productions of a youngster, at the best." [54]

Amateurish they may have been, but Wolfe was so pleased by their reception that he began to dream of the day when he would be able to write plays with professional competence, and his dream was sustained by Koch, who urged him to follow up his work at Chapel Hill with study under prestigious drama professor George Pierce Baker at Harvard.

In the two plays staged by the Carolina Playmakers, and in the other drama experiments essayed in his last two years at Chapel Hill, Wolfe acquired an ear for dialogue, an ability to develop a scene. If their professor was more concerned with folklore than with literary discipline, he nevertheless gave an expansive feeling of self-confidence to Wolfe and his classmates. Warmed by the approbation of Koch's twinkling eyes and his glowing words, each of them believed—for a magical moment, at any rate—that he was a "genius" whose world was his oyster. In soberer moments Wolfe kept his sense of humor, writing in a "Bibliograph":

> It is an excellent thing to watch
> The work of Frederick Henry Koch. . . .
> You'll get right here the artist's thrill,
> The Renaissance of Chapel Hill,
> And soon 'neath every roof and steeple
> You'll hear the "Drammer of the Peepul."
> . . . It is an excellent thing to say
> That thou are [sic] "F. K.'s" protege.[55]

7. Senior

The summer of 1919 in Asheville was a relatively uneventful one for Wolfe. Fred was home from the Navy and went along on a family picnic to Hendersonville, and there in a drugstore he unwittingly lifted a metal chair into a four-bladed ceiling fan. The havoc wreaked on fan and drugstore, to say nothing of the pandemonium among ice-cream-eating customers, brought on a cyclonic uproar of the first degree.[1] From time to time, Wolfe worked out with J. B. McIntosh, championship wrestler, in a barn behind W. O.'s house on Woodfin Street.[2] With that exercise and doubtless with a bit of baseball, his favorite sport, he kept in shape. He saw a lot of Lora French, summer visitor in town, but the relationship was cut short one evening when Wolfe was startled by the appearance of her landlady as the two of them sat together in the yard. Without pausing to say goodbye, he jumped the hedge, tore his trousers, sped off in disarray, and to cover his embarrassment, hastened the next day to visit his sister Effie's family in Anderson. Later he wrote Lora "what a fool he had been to have wasted any time we might have had together."[3]

The university opened in October. When registration was finally completed, there were 1350 students, more than 500 over the number the year before. Almost 95% were from

North Carolina. The largest department, English, enrolled 608, then romance languages 510, chemistry 483, on down to Greek 17 and rural economics 8. Of the 41 women, three each were taking law and medicine, and one was studying electrical engineering.[4] Newly elected President Harry Woodburn Chase greeted the assembled students on October 2, and that evening at Y.M.C.A. College Night in Gerrard Hall, speeches were made by Parson Moss, Dean of Students Frank Graham, Corydon P. Spruill, and Thomas Wolfe, who "unfolded himself in sections and discoursed with much freedom on the topic of college publications, a phase of our community life, he said, 'than which there was none than Wheeler.' "[5]

He was editor of the *Tar Heel*, "highest honor in college, I believe," he wrote his mother. "Everybody runs to me with this and that and I am busy not part of the time but all of it—sleeping five hours is essential but I can't spare any more."[6] Fortunately, he had competent and sympathetic assistants in managing editor John H. Kerr and business manager Nathan G. Gooding.

Most of his classes were taught by old friends: Koch in advanced playwriting, Greenlaw in the English Renaissance, and Williams in logic. In the final spring quarter he unhappily had to forego another English class under Greenlaw to take modern European history, a required course. The first of three quarters of journalism, diverging from the old patterns and strongly indicating Wolfe's developing notions of what he might be doing after graduation, was taught by Richard Hurt Thornton, whom Wolfe impressed "as a very capable youngster with considerable literary ambition" but not "an unusually brilliant student."[7] In the winter and spring the news editing and feature writing classes were conducted by C. Addison Hibbard, an affable and enthusiastic young assistant professor of English from Wisconsin. On the way to Hibbard's class, Wolfe would pick handbills off the telephone poles, then sit in the back of the room to write his assignment on them. Only from Wolfe, it need hardly be said, would Hibbard accept themes in such untidiness.[8] Hibbard's "most vivid recollection" of his student was the morning he "entered a classroom early and found [Wolfe] eating a sandwich from a paper bag and writing in pencil on the empty bag. At the end of the hour when I collected the papers," said Hibbard, "I found Tom's grocery store bag and on it was a sonnet which I believe almost any contemporary poet might have been pleased to write."[9] Wolfe's unconventionality lost him the journalism cup that year to his *Tar Heel* associate Nathan G. Gooding, whose promptness and neatness with assignments were adjudged more worthy of recognition than the irregularities of Wolfe's entries, no matter how talented their content.[10]

At the Pi Kappa Phi house he roomed with Charles M. Hazlehurst, who, though instructor in mathematics and participant in a variety of campus activities, understood and endured Wolfe's habits and peculiarities with more composure than had the succession of roommates the spring before. Wolfe was not unaware of the strain imposed on even the most easygoing companion and wondered about Charles Hazlehurst. "I'll never forget the fortitude he showed in sharing his room with me. Every morning he looked over in the corner at my dirty laundry which mounted like a pyramid from October to Christmas . . . but never a word said he! What moments of unrest I must have caused him! Did he ever stand by my bedside while I was asleep and grit through his teeth: 'God damn you, I'll fix you now!' "[11] After football games Wolfe showed up for informal dancing at the chapter house,[12] and while he never invited a girl of his own to such an occasion, there seemed to be no dearth of partners. Some of the students competed in "The number of girls one may have to a dance—'Beany' Kinlaw and his six—Charles Hazlehurst [*sic*] and his three—'Gre-e-at Day!' "[13]

Evidence of Wolfe's campus-wide popularity was his election by the student body as the senior-class "Student Council man, at large."[14] Oddly enough, at Chapel Hill he was deemed somewhat a prude who favored expulsion from the university for regulation-breakers, noisy brawlers, and rowdy drinkers.[15] The Council, known to the students as the "Carolina Shipping Board," met upstairs at the Y.M.C.A., and when President John Washburn and Wolfe strode simultaneously into the Y, everybody "wondered who was up."[16] Strict as he might seemed to have been, he was nevertheless capable of walking in on a poker game, saying nothing, quickly turning his back and walking out.[17]

If hazing of the traditional sort was contrary to Student Council dictum, Wolfe rationalized an exception at initiations. An invitation to join the literary society Sigma Upsilon, written by Wolfe, was sent to Paul Green. "Tom always liked to be mysterious," said Green, "so he rigged up an initiation that was really something," telling Green to go to the Methodist Church and lie all night between the pews. The six-year-older Green, veteran of the war in France, thought the plan ridiculous and simply didn't go to the church—a dereliction at which Wolfe took such offense that he expressed the opinion that Green ought not to be allowed to join. But Green was given another chance, and the next day received a letter to go to the road beside the cemetery with a box of Nabisco wafers, then run up and down repeating, "Zuzu, Zuzu, I'm a little Zuzu." Green was attempting to comply with the sophomoric foolishness when suddenly Wolfe and several other members jumped from behind a tombstone with "long paddles like barrel staves" and began beating him, Wolfe pounding away hardest in revenge for the church-pew defection. In his soft voice Green said, "Tom, don't hit me any more. I want to be in Sigma Upsilon but don't hit me any more," whereupon Wolfe renewed his attack more fiercely than ever. "For a while, I hated Tom Wolfe," Green says.[18]

Even as Wolfe entered ardently into affairs like this, he

turned up, when he found time to do so, at meetings of the Buncombe County Club, the Y.M.C.A. Cabinet, the Athletic Council, and the Di Society, where he made humorous talks, debated the open-shop policy, and participated in a discussion on America's intervention in Mexico.[19] At a Di smoker on October 18 "Mr. Thomas Wolfe, alias Buck Gavin . . . held the society in breathless suspense with his thrilling stories: 'The Fall of Swine Castle,' 'The Last of the Profiteers,' or 'Sam Holebrows Departure,' ending with the one-act tragedy entitled, 'The Streets of Durham, or Dirty Work at Cross Roads,' "[20] a wildly incoherent vaudeville-act jumble mostly in dramatic form. This mixture of popular quotation, songs, melodramatic exclamations, and prose in ballad measures was printed in the *Carolina Tar Baby*,[21] campus humor magazine, under its extended title "The Streets of Durham, or Dirty Work at the Cross Roads (A Tragedy in Three Muddy Acts) by Tommy Wolfe." The disrupted conditions of Durham streets then being paved was in Wolfe's eyes only an outlandish botch, and the multiple short scenes of his skit allowed an assorted group of characters, quickly appearing and as quickly disappearing, to have their say and sing their songs: policemen, Trinity College students, "belles," the *Tar Heel* editor himself, to say nothing of Father Time, History, and "John Q. Asphalt, a scheming contractor and his co-conspirator, Nemesis, the steam shovel." As Thanksgiving was approaching, the sketch giddily concluded with a Thanksgiving hymn. The delight of Wolfe and his friends in absurdity perhaps accounts for the jaunty and defenseless turbulence of the piece, or Wolfe may have simply dashed it off, said Corydon P. Spruill, "without point just to confuse the readers, Wolfe being the sort who would do that."[22] The *Tar Baby*, revived after six years with its lone purpose to air such nonsense as "The Streets of Durham," listed Wolfe on its Advisory Board, along with John Terry, Albert Coates, Moses Rountree, and Professor Greenlaw. Though Wolfe was on the staff of the *Magazine*, its ancient and lordly competitor, as assistant editor-in-chief, his play "Concerning Honest Bob," coming late in the year, was his only contribution to a journal now committed, in high seriousness and solemnity, to printing local-color "folk" poems and stories by such writers as LeGette Blythe and Paul Green.

Meanwhile, his editorship of the *Tar Heel* involved him almost totally. At staff meetings around a big table on the second floor of the Y, Wolfe—"sprawled all over one end of the table, with numerous papers before him, [running] his hands thru his unusually heavy mop of hair"—assigned news stories to his assistants, but sought no help or advice on editorials,[23] practically all of which he wrote himself in accordance with an erratic procedure becoming more and more routine. With his pockets full of scraggly notes, some of them written on match box covers,[24] he would pop through the door of managing editor John Kerr's dormitory room at Pettigrew 6 shortly before all copy for the weekly edition was due, and there he would "write editorials in longhand and remake and rewrite much of the remainder of the paper. Kerr, a very methodical person, was nearly driven to distraction."[25] If a typewriter was at hand, Wolfe would peck out copy with two fingers.[26] When the copy did not suit him, he revised it leisurely, undisturbed about deadlines, and all too frequently the paper came out on Sunday instead of Saturday. More in the realm of Wolfe legend than actuality is the story of his asking J. S. Massenburg, an assistant manager, "How's the copy today, Jimmy?" "No copy, Tom." At which fructuous Tom Wolfe sits up all night, and by morning has an entire issue ready for the press.[27]

Though Wolfe off and on thought of himself as a sportswriter, as attested by a fragment left among his papers,[28] his enthusiasm for athletics was sporadic. When word came to him that the *Tar Heel's* failure to support the football team was one of the reasons for its mediocre season, he angrily burst into Albert Coates's room on November 7 and told him, "I'm going to cover the ball game tomorrow and see that the *Tar Heel* does support the team." On Saturday he sat in the stands at Emerson Field and watched the Virginia Military Institute defeat the University of North Carolina 29–7. His write-up was a marvel of rhapsodic support, as in sentences like these: "Mr. Leach, who attends school at V. M. I., would grab the ball and race 40 yards up the field when Carolina's unpregnable [*sic*] defense would stiffen and throw him for a loss. Then Mr. Leach would go around end for 15 yards only to run against the same obstacle as before. Before defense such as this V.M.I. was helpless and was held to a baggardly [*sic*] 29 points." On Monday morning after the game, Dean Frank Graham suggested at chapel that a student pep rally might help matters (dispel the gloom, perhaps?), and so that afternoon Wolfe, still in a mood to support the team, joined G. D. Crawford in leading the students in cheers, then swept with them down to the athletic field where the players were understandably having less than a spirited practice, gave a new series of "long lusty yells . . . and began a snake dance around the field, which is emblematic of victory and not defeat."[29] The following Saturday the team won over Davidson College 10–0.

Though Wolfe's sprightly and well-written editorials did not neglect sportsmanship and team loyalty, the emphasis was elsewhere. During the fall he plugged the Campus Cabinet, the publications, the literary societies, the honor system, and spoke out against drinking at college dances and "rowdyism by students at public meetings or entertainments." He piously defined "the Carolina Spirit" as embodying "three great attributes of a man's make-up—the Gentleman, Honor, and Manhood."[30] With such high-toned language at his command, no wonder the faculty, as he boastfully wrote his mother, said that his editorials had had a "steadying influence on campus this unsettled year."[31]

One of Wolfe's most enjoyable duties as editor was the mandatory trip to Durham every week to block out the *Tar Heel* at the Seeman Printery on Corcoran Street. When a representative of the Trinity College *Chronicle* was present, he would twit the fellow by declaring that printing of the "Chronic-Ill" could be put aside for the present; "it wasn't worth printing anyway."[32] If, in measuring out his copy to fit the allotted pages, Wolfe had several galleys left over, he debonairly made room for them by throwing out the advertisements. Voluntary subscriptions to the *Tar Heel* from only 250 students were obviously inadequate to finance the paper, and the ads, secured by business manager Nathan G. Gooding through long hours and hard work, constituted a necessary source of revenue. It was Gooding's out-of-pocket responsibility to pay Seeman, and Wolfe's wayward habits irked him, but he did not mention the matter to Wolfe, who he knew would never understand that editorials and good copy were not more essential than financially necessary advertisements. On Gooding's hands at the end of the year was a $400 personal debt.[33]

Ernest Seeman and others at the print shop were fond of Wolfe, often inviting him over to "a Greek beanery nearby known as the Royal Cafe." On one occasion, when Wolfe had two students along with him, Seeman "sensed that this very slender and shy mountaineer Wolfe was the natural center of gravity," for his friends set up a "flow of banter and repartee & wisecrack . . . hoping to bait him into talking (they seemed to want to 'show him off' as a natural curiosity; as something beyond their understanding, tho secretly by them admired). At last they succeeded. One of them asked: 'Say, Tom, when you get to be a famous writer are you going to use your middle initial or just sign "Tom Wolfe"?' His bright & sensitive young face gave off a shrewd and amused & somewhat scornful smile, and he replied: 'Hell no; how would it look if Shakspere had signed his stuff "William J. Shakspere"?' "[34]

Sometimes his *Tar Heel* business kept him in Durham later than the last jitney run to Chapel Hill. On the street one night about ten o'clock he happened upon Jerome Pence, whom he immediately began begging to walk with him back to the university. At first Pence, who was planning to stay overnight in Durham, took it as a joke, but when he "became aware of the fact that Tom was serious about walking," he wrote, "I just couldn't persuade myself to go in for such an undertaking, knowing full well that walking for him meant running for me, if I intended to keep up. However, he attempted to assure me that he would let me set the pace and about 11:30 P.M. we set out. Before we reached the cemetery in West Durham, my tongue was hanging out, and about 1 A.M. we stopped on the *halfway bridge* to rest. About 2:30 A.M. we were plodding up Strowd's Hill, and the worst downpour I've felt descended on us. Tom left me at his fraternity house down next to the Presbyterian Church." Pence limped across campus to find a bed.[35]

The big event of the autumn was the Thanksgiving Day football game with the University of Virginia, played for the first time in Chapel Hill. Special trains came in from Goldsboro, Winston-Salem, and Charlotte; faculty wives served luncheon in Swain Hall and the University Inn; nine thousand spectators watched as Virginia was defeated 6–0; and that night to the music of a Philadelphia orchestra playing in the Big Four Warehouse in Durham, students and their girls danced at the Carolina-Virginia Ball. Editorially Wolfe noted that Virginia "fought fiercely and died gamely" and that the Carolina students, "though delirious with the joy of winning, never once forgot the courtesy that was due the defeated team."[36]

Two weeks after the excitement, the *Tar Heel* carried a reminiscent essay, "Ye Who Have Been There Only Know,"[37] in which Wolfe recalled the Richmond game of his freshman year: the frantic arrangements, the all-night trip in a day coach, the dawn arrival in the city, the rallies, the game, the celebrations, the sleepy ride home. While most of Wolfe's poems, short stories, plays, and other writings during his Chapel Hill years are little more than the work of a competent, frequently talented student in a rush to complete an assignment, "Ye Who Have Been There Only Know" foreshadows the mature Wolfe in its exuberance and nostalgia, in its expression of his "quivering anticipation" and "feverish delight" as the train headed northward.[38]

On the evening of the very Saturday when the *Tar Heel* carrying the essay was distributed, a less than inspired aspect of versatile undergraduate Wolfe was made palpable as he stalked the Carolina Playmakers stage acting his own Captain Richard Harkins, "degenerate Southern gentleman" in "The Third Night: A Mountain Play of the Supernatural."

In December he wrote his mother that *Tar Heel* matters would keep him on campus after the other students had left for the Christmas holidays. "It's hard, I know, but you must pay dearly for college honors. . . . Do you want me home? . . . I'll need $70. . . . If you think best I stay here deduct expense home and send rest."[39] Evidently the money was sent, for at the fraternity house Donnell Van Noppen remembered "Tom packing up to go home for Christmas; from underneath the bed, underneath the dresser, and out of the dresser drawers he pulled all sorts of dirty clothes, threw them in the trunk, stood up on them, stamped them down and closed the trunk and he was ready to go. Upon his return, Tom would look comparatively dressed up, but within a week afterwards it was the same old Tom."[40]

In January Wolfe changed rooms for the last time, moving across Franklin Street from the Pi Kappa Phi house to the University Inn, a ramshackle, tree-shaded, wooden building, gray with age and neglect. In a second-story corner room, heated by a tin stove, Wolfe took up quarters with a friend from whom he had borrowed the $10 deposit.[41] When weather permitted, they spent the night just outside their doorway on a broad sleeping porch overlooking Alumni Hall, where Horace Williams expounded on the meaning of "the *Begriff*" before young North Carolinians still wet behind the ears. Albert Coates and Dougald MacMillan had a room close by, and Clement Eaton was next door. They were quiet, studious men, disturbed more often than they wished by the arrival of Wolfe, who immediately became the "center of assorted debates, colloquia and hullabaloos."[42] It was as it had always been. At the Inn Wolfe spurned the small dining room and continued to preside from his accustomed seat at the head of a table in Swain Hall, his appetite enormous and his "manners Rabelaisian."[43]

But no matter, for Wolfe was a Big Man on Campus, always ready to talk, always cordial. No matter if days passed without his taking off his clothes,[44] if his shoes squeaked and he did not shave.[45] A joke going the rounds has C. R. Sumner say, "Look here, Tom, why the devil don't you get a haircut?" Wolfe explains, "That's one way I save money. All I have to do is to let my pants get baggy and my hair long and they think I'm a genius."[46] A man of genius smoked a pipe, he decided, and so Corydon P. Spruill took his picture—his pants baggy but his hair decently cut—with an unaccustomed pipe at his lips.[47]

He started off the day at "Swine" Hall on "tough steak and cold grits," attended his classes, especially the Horace Williams head-swimmer in "Aluminum Building," ate lunch and went to the post office, passed the afternoon working on the *Tar Heel*, at "supper" found "a rubber heel with gravy in side dish," repaired to the University Inn where "kindling wood was industriously split up and down hall outside door," then accompanied by an acquaintance (movie-goers never went alone) toted his bag of peanuts into the Pickwick Theater to slaughter any student so unwise as to leave himself open to assault. With peace restored after the peanut battles, the screen flickered with the glamorous figures of Theda Bara,

Douglas Fairbanks, Dorothy Gish, John Barrymore, or Gloria Swanson. Attendance at the Pickwick was more regular than at Collier Cobb's geology class, a reporter observed, and students wondered why they couldn't get credit for it. "They never look at the posters of announcements," he wrote. "It matters little to them who is on, and at what stage of the picture they enter." Thus it was nothing short of downright disaster when a mild influenza epidemic hit the community in mid-February and closed down the Pickwick. The postponement of the Carolina Playmakers' production of *The Importance of Being Earnest* was viewed with less alarm.[48]

On occasional evenings students gathered around the white columns of the Old Well and listened to a "string orchestra, playing a strange combination of jazz and sad melodies."[49] At the ensuing bull sessions Wolfe and his companions took up where they had left off that morning in Horace Williams's class. "We discussed the idea of God most earnestly: truth, goodness, beauty were our meat."[50]

Wolfe's life at this intoxicated time, he wrote Ben Cone nine years later, "was as close to magic as I've ever been."[51]

There were secret, more tranquil hours. "The desire for isolation when one had a bowel action," he wrote in the Autobiographical Outline—"Late on a cool chill night (or a night in Spring) when all the world has gone to bed to feel the seductive thrill of its approach, particularly when one has written well, to restrain in gently, to submit to its growing ecstasies; and finally to submit—The isolation of wind and snow and rain." And Wolfe remembered "The Library—The quiet rooms—the general discomfort and inaccessibility of books—Lord Bacon in the huge bindings." And he reflected on "Masturbation . . . It opens to you the kingdoms of the earth—A picture—a mistress—A painting—flesh—a leg upon a street—the glances of an eye in a restaurant—or 'Thank you, no. Not to-day'—all are yours—Every Man His Own Harem—No need for a perpetual mistress."[52]

In the dusty world of grimy magic was the Malbourne Hotel in Durham—"Caught . . . by Mr. Bugg [the manager]—The whore with the Silver dollars—My companion who 'went first' —The Belmont hotel at Raleigh." And "The woman in Durham at the Station hotel—The Southern bawd—a Negro porter—The hours of waiting in a rancid room—The descent—on to a cold back porch—Entrance to her room—A year later on the dissecting boards at Chapel Hill—The world hardened on a harlot's face," and "The wrung loins of boyhood—I weep for lost virginity. Is it not as painful in a boy as in a girl?"[53]

No great distance separated Wolfe of the Malbourne Hotel and Wolfe of the Golden Fleece, as he met with Albert Coates, Jeff Bynum, Nathan Mobley, Clement Eaton, Nathan G. Gooding, Corydon P. Spruill, and several others to select members for that most revered order. In Gerrard Hall, where the tapping ceremony was witnessed for the first time by the student body, Wolfe sat with other Big Men on Campus to hear a patriotic, visionary address by Thomas Walter Bickett, Governor of North Carolina. Among the eight new members were John Kerr, William H. Bobbitt, and President Harry Woodburn Chase.[54] About the subsequent "initiation—joyous and cruel," Wolfe especially remembered President Chase, "A grown man blindfolded waiting to be 'taken in' to an honorary *student's* organization—What passes through his head?"[55]

Wolfe's self-assurance, now well developed, and his consequent brashness sometimes betrayed him and belied his otherwise adroit conduct in campus matters. At the Carolina Smoker in Swain Hall on March 9—"With Noise Makers, Confetti, Eats and Near Artists," with Professor Collier Cobb as toastmaster, with Jazz Band, Wrestling Match, Mandolin Club, Glee Club, a stunt by the Satyrs, and Eats, Eats, Eats[56] —no deviation from the expected came when "The Right Learned Thomas Clayton Wolfe, in a short but wittily eloquent harangue, proposed a toast to the townspeople and the faculty." [57] It was as it had always been. But at the Senior Smoker on March 31, [58] the night after the Golden Fleece tapping, when called on to introduce Archibald Henderson, Wolfe was deserted by his normal good sense of propriety. Professor Henderson, esteemed mathematician and famed biographer of George Bernard Shaw, was not only one of the most important and influential members of the faculty, but an archly dignified aristocrat in looks and manner. "When I learned that I was to introduce Dr. Henderson," Wolfe said to the assemblage, "I went over to the mathematics department to get some information about him. 'You came to the wrong place,' they told me. 'Dr. Henderson is a literary man, not a mathematician. You should go to the English department.' I went over there and they said, 'You came to the wrong place. Dr. Henderson is not a literary man. He is a mathematician. You should go to the Mathematics department.'" Wolfe casually mentioned Henderson's book on Shaw. "And now I want to introduce a man, who, among the literati, is known as one of the world's greatest mathematicians, and among the mathematicians is known as one of the world's greatest literary figures." [59] Restrained laughter.

It was not a new joke in Chapel Hill, but one repeated always in private, and Henderson's eyes glinted, barely perceptibly, at the whippersnapper's effrontery and impertinence; then quickly he recovered his composure and addressed the students. Perhaps only gradually did Wolfe connect his churlish introduction of Henderson with the portrait-hanging incident and other discourtesies under which he had cringed during his freshman days. Four years after leaving Chapel Hill he wrote Henderson of the time "I had the honor to be paired with you on the speaking program of a senior smoker of the class of 1920. It was my function to introduce you, and I did, using the good natured, but somewhat ill-considered, slap stick which finds favor on a campus. I referred to your connection with Shaw, and spelled his name 'Pshaw.' I think you were not deeply offended, but when you spoke a note of reverence entered your voice as you said his name. I have a devilish memory which recalls past folly, my young crudities, my lapses from good taste, and makes me rue them. And I have often thought of that occasion with pain and regret. . . ."[60]

Such wrong-headed moments were rare. Based on his editorials in the *Tar Heel*, Wolfe's image was that of an upright, crusading, idealistic young man who could never be guilty of unmannerliness, indiscretion, or covert trips to Durham and Raleigh. On the editorial page he pleaded for courtesy at athletic contests, for more new university buildings; he proposed organized snowball contests between classes instead of haphazard side-taking; he lamented overcrowding in student quarters; he applauded Clean Up Week and the Golden Fleece innovation of tapping new members in public ceremony; in "This Is No Place for Thieves" he castigated marauders in dormitories and laboratories; he congratulated victorious debate teams, praised the Carolina Spirit, and bemoaned the small attendance for Metropolitan Opera contralto Sophie Braslau in Memorial Hall; he even wrote a glowing appreciation of Parson Moss.[61]

When the state gubernatorial campaign heated up in late winter, he became interested in politics. Paul Green, who sat with him for a political address by candidate O. Max Gardner on February 25, remembers that Wolfe snickered, "Sweetened wind—that's all" as they left the building.[62] Gardner's abundant life" speech nettled him as "the beautiful prose of President Graham sometimes bored him."[63] His "Useful Advice to Candidates" became his most often quoted editorial:

Mr. O. Max Gardner's address to the student body on Wednesday night marks the beginning of a series of addresses to be made here by all the Democratic candidates for Governor, and the Republicans, also, if they can be brought here. Thus does the University step boldly into the arena of impartial politics and gives the pleasant challenge to these gentlemen to come here and show their wares. Not having had time to prepare our invaluable little booklet, "Handbook of Useful Information to those Gubernatorially Inclined, Who Will Speak at Chapel Hill," we beg to herewith append a few admonitions that may be useful to them.

1. Remember that you are speaking to a fair-minded, impartial group of men, who have small respect for petty appeals of a partisan nature.

2. Remember that you will be hospitably and courteously received, whether we approve of you or not. It is therefore your own fault if you don't appear to your best advantage.

3. Tell us something we don't already know. We will agree quite freely that the Old North State is the peer of them all and that the labor situation is serious. But if you will come boldly forward and exhibit two or three planks out of your platform that shows [*sic*] you have been doing some real thinking on your own part, we will have more respect for you, no matter if we don't all agree with you.

4. And remember lastly, gentlemen, that you yourself will be either the vindication or condemnation to your claims for the Governorship. We are interested in you, the man; in the evidences of your own individuality and not in your party politics. You find us with minds open, receptive and unprejudiced; in the one brief hour that is yours before us we'll make our decision about you, and the tag we put upon you is likely to be the right one. Yours with kindness and friendship.—The Student Body.[64]

If university administrators at first felt considerably apprehensive about the effect such outspokenness might conceivably have on future legislative appropriations, they must have felt pride when the editorial caught on and was reprinted all over the state.[65] Yet it seems not to have had much influence on candidate Cameron Morrison, who on March 10 in Gerrard Hall flayed the Republicans and exhorted the students to examine the "fundamental fabrics of the Democratic party as portrayed in Jefferson, Monroe and Vance."[66] In the same issue with his "Useful Advice to Candidates"—for Wolfe could not long remain solemn—was the *"Tar Heel's* State Ticket," including jitney-driver C. S. Pendergraft as candidate for state treasurer, and Thomas Clinkscales Wolfe for judge of the Third Judicial District.

With the state gubernatorial campaign out of the way, Wolfe turned to campus politics. He deplored "political rings" and "confidential talks," "personal attacks," and dormitory canvassing at night. He had only scorn for the hypocrisy of men running for office who considered it brazen and unbecoming to say so. Two or more campus political organizations were needed, with candidates and their supporters announcing platforms and conducting campaigns "in an open manner."[67] His editorial temper was reflected in "Concerning Honest Bob," the last play he wrote at Chapel Hill.

For its April 10 number the staff of the *Tar Baby* appointed Wolfe "editor of this issue," its forty-four pages, except for advertisements and exchanges, burlesquing the *News and Observer*, widely read Raleigh daily newspaper. Wolfe had contributed to the humor magazine with some regularity since its revival the preceding autumn. Though "The Streets of Durham" carried his by-line, other entries cannot be positively identified. Probably Wolfe's, however, is a dialogue among Raleigh-bound students when their automobile breaks down and The Agnostic joyously spies "the University truck just heaving into sight o'er yon cosmic hill." The parody smacks confidently of Wolfe, as does "Durham Dramatic Drippings," a column of news about the Carolina Haymakers and Frederick H. Notch, "aged dean of folk minstrelsy," whose "male star this year is the rising young dramatist T. Clayton Woolfe, who enacts the leading role in his own play, 'White Lightnin',' of folk life in Western Carolina. Mr. Woolfe, although scarcely more than 14 years of age, is a stalwart youth from the mountains of North Carolina and is well over six feet in his stocking feet. He appears wearing boots. The tragic finality of his great line, 'The soup is served,' sends an electric thrill through the footlights."[68] At caricature like this, of the Carolina Playmakers as well as of himself, Wolfe was by now an old hand.

Though the legend persists that he "sat up all night and wrote the entire forty-four pages" of the April 10 *Tar Baby*,[69] such inventiveness and industry were simply not possible. As a matter of fact, he accepted the assignment seriously, determined to do his best so as not to disappoint its 4500 readers.[70] He had help, too, for as he told Lora French, "I edited this issue and, in fact, wrote most of the stuff,"[71] thus disclaiming credit for all the copy. In preparation Wolfe went to Raleigh, followed reporter Ben Dixon MacNeill of the *News and Observer* on his afternoon beat of state departments and, with time out to eat, pored over files of the newspaper, note paper in hand, till after midnight. At three in the morning, when MacNeill told Wolfe he was leaving, Wolfe muttered he'd go along with him. He slept soundly in MacNeill's room, arose at eight, thanked MacNeill and, noticing a copy of Baudelaire's *Flowers of Evil* with the Beardsley drawings, told MacNeill, "Think I'll take this along. Send it back to you sometime."[72] Notes stuffed in his pockets, Wolfe returned to Chapel Hill, but he never, of course, sent back the book.

Lenoir Chambers declared that in the burlesque *Tar Baby* "the make-up of the News and Observer has been copied as accurately as printing conditions allowed."[73] But of more interest to its readers was Wolfe's lampooning of news items and feature departments. Among the foreign dispatches was an item from Petrograd on the Homecoming of Brother Lenin: "His friends turned out to welcome him and shot 47 conservatives for his delectation. It was a grand old homecoming, a mighty tribute to the chief of the Soviet, and tears filled his eyes as he thanked them for the entertainment." In Greensboro, Mrs. Lem E. Hitem told police after shooting her husband, "He drank his tea from a saucer. I could stand his tyranny no longer." At a revival meeting by evangelist Hurricane Mack Mackintosh in Raleigh, "twenty-seven women fainted, thirty-three became hysterical and had to be carried off, and seventeen strong members of the pipe-fitters' union broke down and sobbed when the parson spoke of 'crooked joints.' " On her deathbed Mrs. Emma Levinsky of Raleigh "cautioned her son against the evils of dime novels, chewing gum, and the insidious soda fountain. 'Patrick, avoid all these things and, above all, let the *News and Observer* be your guide through life. I shall not fear for you then.' "

Wolfe included Letters to the Editor, a poem by Edgar A. Guessed, comics, and an episode from the serialized novel "The Easier Weigh" by Irwin S. Slobb. In the Society section, "Zeb McCracken drove in from Cary . . . and took us by surprise, paying his back subscription from 1893 to 1902, inclusive. Hit us again, Zeb." Among the Want Ads was "WANTED—MAN OF ALL WORK BY a widow lady to do light house work. Cary P.D.Q. Box 78." In the sports news Davidson College lost to "Peace [a Raleigh girls' school] in a Very Fast Game of Post Office," and Carolina was getting ready for a baseball game with the visiting Bryn Mawr team and had "its entire force of campus workers getting the athletic fields in shape, but unfortunately the force was cut in half yesterday when one of them was taken sick." A filler let it be known that "Ladies in Patagonia are wearing shorter beads this year than ever before." In a testimonial for the patent medicine "Tanbark," a Charlotte man stated: "For some years I have had a fair sized wart on the back of my neck which I have been in the habit of using as a collar button.

After taking two bottles of Tanbark, I now hang my pants on it." The Witless McBoob Company—"Everything In Attire For Growing Girruls"—recommended its popular merchandise "Ladies Thingermabobs" varying from pale pink for the high school miss to serpent-eye green for the village vamp.

Not only could Wolfe dispense a folk humor of parody, exaggeration, paradox, and wisecrack, but he was also a natural target for it. A snapshot on the cover of his burlesque *Tar Baby* pictured a young man with his arm around a girl under the announcement "O. I. Saye to Wed Hillsboro Girl." William Polk often spun out a story of how the girl's irate parents encountered Wolfe and threatened to sue him for libel. Wolfe rose from his chair, all six feet four and 178 pounds of him accumulated in only nineteen years, and replied, "You can't sue me." "Why not?" demanded the parents. "Because I'm a minor."—Another yarn has a "Freshman approaching Tom Wolfe one day last fall immediately upon the opening of the University. 'Mister, are you President Chase?' 'Look a-here, sonny,' roared Tom, as he caught the Fresh by the ear and faced him toward the gym. 'You go see Dr. Lawson; I'm Buck Gavin and the law'll git you in the end.' "—During the football season, a new student remarked to the coach, "It sure is a great pity and loss to the varsity that Tom Wolfe doesn't play football." Coach Campbell wanted to know why? "He could fall down with the ball and make a touchdown every time."—In March perhaps it was Wolfe himself who inserted among the otherwise routine "personals" in the *Tar Heel* this startling news: "Thomas Clayton Wolfe, editor of the Tar Heel, was on the Hill a few fleeting hours last Wednesday. Mr. Wolfe is taking a rest cure in Raleigh and Greensboro following a week of strenuous and nerve-racking examinations. It is thought that he is taking the Keeley cure [for alcoholics]."[74]

The four undergraduate Chapel Hill years were steadily moving toward their end. At a "hallelujah meeting" in chapel to celebrate recent athletic and debate victories, "Tom Wolfe, as chairman, reviewed the events won by Carolina." For the Senior Class cabaret-banquet some days later, "Tom of the Mountains" promised to provide "a rare bit of amusement." [75] It was as it had always been. And so habit-forming had it become for everyone to solicit his participation that, even in those last weeks, the Y.M.C.A. chose him to plan for the work of a "Boys" department the following autumn, and Albert Coates appointed him as one of the representatives of the student body to draft recommendations for the proposed Graham Memorial building. [76]

In these hurried hours, did busy, energetic, popular, prominent Tom of the Mountains spare even a moment to assess the past four years? Had he done so, there were a few conclusions he might have reached. He was no top student, even though in the three quarters of his senior year he had a string of gentleman's B's with two A's in Hibbard's journalism and an A in Williams's Logic. Four years back, he had come to the university with the hazy, superficial purpose of preparing himself for life, as the expression went, never more than minimally committed to his father's plan that he take law, and knowing full well that he would "grievously" disappoint him. By May of 1920 he had long felt inside him "the stirrings of a desire to write," evasive perhaps. "I told myself," Wolfe confessed, "that I wanted to go into journalism . . . because newspaper work provided me with the only means I knew whereby I could, in some fashion, write, and earn a living." [77] But his friend Paul Green looked more perceptively at Wolfe than the outward-going senior could look at himself, and Green recognized there the beginnings of a "terrific ache and hunger and impetuous reach. And always associated with it in his last college days . . . was the desire to be a playwright." [78] Wolfe did not then know what he came to know—"that writing is the most painful and exhausting work on earth." [79]

Wolfe's Chapel Hill experience was a germinal and productive one, compounded with "love and affection" for a campus of "unpaved streets which become pools of mud when it rains."[80] Indeed the university was, as his father believed, "a kind of magic door" opening "to a man not only all the reserves of learning" but providing him, it was thought, with "a kind of magic key to the great material rewards of place and money."[81] Wolfe was happy there, loyally if sometimes questioningly accepting its customs and traditions and beliefs. The South was, after all, everything he knew, and his Menckenian critical attitudes did not surface till "The Sahara of the Bozart" gave expression to antipathies dormant and unsuspected, and till years of residence in the North permitted him to develop perspective from a distance.

If he detected crucial flaws and weaknesses in Bernard, Greenlaw, Koch, and Williams while at Chapel Hill, no evidence hints of it. If he laughed at his own folkplays, if he exploited "the *Begriff*" in comical exchange, it was merely his good humor, his careful program after his freshman year not to let his classmates observe that he might be taking himself seriously. It is a pose adopted by hundreds of thousands of undergraduates everywhere. What is important is that there in that Southern wilderness, under Bernard, Greenlaw, Koch, and Williams, he flourished like a palm tree in Arcadia. Bernard taught him a classic Greek humanism and an approach he might conceivably take toward life. Greenlaw touched his romantic side and gave him tools and substance. Koch pointed out work to be done and inspired him with faith in himself as creator. But it was Williams who stirred his brain. Whatever may be said of Wolfe's professors at Chapel Hill— that they failed to discipline him, that they confused him concerning the difference between life and literature, that they provided him with no training in philosophical orderliness—at least they did not try to remake him. They did not curb him as they did other students—and how destructive it would have been!—but accepted him as he was, with confidence and belief. In allowing him to race against himself at his chosen speed, they were wise, enlightened men.

On Friday, May 28, Wolfe's class held the first of four meetings at Davie Poplar, tradition-marked tree under which it was said General William Richardson Davie rested in 1792 when searching for a university site and looking at the green splendor all about him, exclaimed, "This is it!" At the second gathering, Nathan G. Gooding called for the resignation of acting class president John P. Washburn, Wolfe's erstwhile accomplice on the "Carolina Shipping Board," for being drunk and disorderly the preceding Sunday morning. Class vice president Ben Cone took charge.[82] Examinations were held through June 11. In the annual *Yackety Yack*, Wolfe's eleven lines of small print listing his undergraduate activities and honors were far more than those for any other student, just as his three "superlatives"—Best Writer, Most Original, Wittiest[83]—outnumbered the encomiums voted his classmates. In a descriptive paragraph below his photograph, Nathan Mobley[84] wrote that Buck Wolfe could "do more between 8:25 and 8:30 than the rest of us can do all day, and it is no wonder that he is classed as a genius."[85]

Though there had been less and less correspondence between Chapel Hill and Asheville, Wolfe's family rose to the momentous occasion of Commencement. Brother Fred wrote that he intended coming if he could get away.[86] Mrs. Wolfe brought down proud W. O., who was of the notion, so out of touch was the sick man with what had happened in the last few years, that his son was now ready to go into politics.[87] "Papa's illness during commencement—Complaint against the heat—On his last legs but with two more years to live—The room I found for them . . . The suit I bought in Durham—Chase's whispered word to papa."[88] After the baccalaureate sermon on Sunday, June 13, W. O. heard Wolfe's presentation of the class gift on Monday morning, and that afternoon at 5:30 during "Closing Exercises of the Senior Class Under

Davie Poplar,"[89] his reading of the sentimental class poem "1920 Says a Few Words to Carolina," in which Wolfe looked ahead to the day when members of his class would

> think again of this night here
> And of these old brown walls,
> Of white old well, and of old South
> With bell's deep booming tone,
> They'll think again of Chapel Hill and—
> Thinking—come back home.[90]

Wolfe feared that his father would be too weak to be present at more than a few of the exercises and, according to Frank Graham, "made engagements" for his mother "well in advance." Mrs. Wolfe was escorted to the Senior Ball by Graham, who recalled "Tom's tender appreciation of his mother" as he brought his date over to speak to them where they sat together. Graham remembered Mrs. Wolfe's pleasure in seeing her son, dressed in formal clothes, "enjoy himself."[91] W. O. was unable to attend the graduation exercises on Wednesday morning to hear the address by Roland S. Morris, American ambassador to Japan. Among the 165 receiving diplomas, in addition to Wolfe, were Nathan Mobley and Corydon P. Spruill. John Terry completed his second year of medicine.[92]

"I hate to leave this place," Wolfe wrote Lora French. "It's mighty hard. It's the oldest state university and there's an atmosphere here that's fine and good."[93] He arranged for his father and mother to return to Asheville, and then, according to Jonathan Daniels—with Wolfe's Student Council "duties of moral supervision" over—"we had a gay party around a bottle of pure white whiskey in one of the half-empty dormitories."[94] It was time to go, but Wolfe still lingered. There was one last mission. Only after seeing Horace Williams was he willing, perhaps suddenly and precipitously, to tear himself away.

8. Horace Williams

Perhaps Wolfe wished to remain forever in that Arcadian retreat, but by now his reluctant leave-taking had become merely an indulgence. Resolved to perform the final rite, he directed his steps, if implication can be trusted, down the paths to the old house and Horace Williams. Assuming that they met, what did they say to each other? Doubtless the occasion was too tense to allow more than the expected amenities. "And when, Mr. Wolfe, will you leave us? And what will you do?" "Tomorrow morning. And yes, I hope to go to Harvard to study playwriting." But these words are of course supposititious.

There was nothing supposititious about Horace Williams, one-man philosophy department and a famous name in North Carolina. Famous he was, too, in Chapel Hill—for his egotism, his eccentricity, and his difficult, contentious nature. "My boys," as he called his students, were his one consuming love. He took pride in quietly boasting that Wolfe was "one of six remarkable students in my thirty years experience here,"[1] an opinion perhaps based on exaggerated prejudice, but at least compensated for by Wolfe's reciprocal devotion. In Williams he found what he had been looking for, "a madman with slakeless thirst," he wrote. "Greenlaw might have done it—

but his mind under the regulation of formal scholarship—
devouring hunger but formalized—What I needed was spirit
that knew no reason."[2]

In January, 1919, Wolfe had registered for Philosophy 15,
A Study of Forces That Shape Life, hardly more than an un-
ashamed confusion of metaphysical commonplaces from Socrates on through to Hegel and contemporary ethics. So icono-
clastic was Williams in his classes, so heatedly did he pursue
his special brand of Socratic probing, that students began to
think he "looked like Socrates and talked like him,"[3] and
then he "Sometimes stopped being Socrates in order to imi-
tate the foes of Socrates—who made the 'lesser side appear the
best.'" Williams incited disagreement if for no other reason
than to fire up the lethargic minds in his classroom. He was
"the magnificent twister," made startling declarations, and
pleaded for "The asking of questions—An old but crafty
boxer, leading you on, turning the laugh on you, laughing
finally at you with the dry husky laugh—Mr. Wolfe, who lies
awake o' nights thinking of things, the flood of feeling on
Mr. Wolfe's face."[4] And Wolfe, sitting on the back row,[5]
took him on, but the Old Man rarely lost any contest, even
those which initially seemed walkovers to Wolfe.

Indeed, this "spirit that knew no reason" was "a subtle and
many-prismed personality," and afterwards, remembering
the class, Wolfe wrote to Williams of how the "years dropped
away like magic: I saw the room in Alumni again in all its
detail, heard the shifting accents of your voice as you would
say one thing or another; see the whole spectacle . . . , your
hand upon one hip, as you looked steadfastly out the window
before the lecture began. It was a wonderful,—an uncanny
experience."[6]

On every first class day, Williams assigned texts and other
readings, but that was the end of it. He never inquired thereafter what philosophers his students were studying, for they
were required only to think, think, think, and become their

own philosophers. Standard philosophies were meaningless unless they became one's own. "We read nothing," Wolfe recalled. "We began to feel certain contempt for people who did read—Science got facts—not principles—unable to solve its own problems—A monster unable to stop its own work—Had raised questions, but was unable to answer them."[7]

Williams's lectures might seem to have had a certain sameness about them, but when discussion arose, the class resembled more "a free-for-all debating club."[8] Discussion was essential, for no truth could be reached until ideas had wrestled with each other.[9] In truth, Williams thought of himself as a Socrates, "a midwife, an accoucheur to young minds giving birth to their ideas."[10] And the young minds, excited and energized as vague abstractions became manifest, were led gloriously by Williams "to the mountain top."[11] As soon as Wolfe established himself in the classroom, Williams "seemed to direct his words" toward him,[12] singling him out with a special attention reserved only for the local demigods.

"I never give an 'A' grade unless a fellow has earned it," Williams declared. "It is an event when a man makes an 'A' in philosophy."[13] Perhaps so. But on one occasion, when Wolfe was reminded of a paper due the next day, he exclaimed, "Oh Lord, I forgot all about it!" and promptly went off to the Pickwick, began writing his assignment, as usual, at bedtime, and "made a better grade than his classmate, who had worked on his for weeks."[14] In Wolfe's five courses under Williams, he received three B's and two A's. "Nat Mobley called me Hegel," Wolfe remembered.[15]

Wolfe devoured metaphysical theories ravenously. "We were deep in philosophy at Chapel Hill," he wrote, "—we juggled about such formidable terms as 'concepts,' 'moments of negation,' and so on, in a way that would have made Spinoza blush; and if I do say so, I was no slouch at it myself . . . [and] could lead with a 'concept' and counter with a 'moment of negation' . . . [and] could split a hair with the best of them."[16] Concepts were the campus rage, and it didn't make any difference "what kind of concept it [happened] to be, a concept of the origin of species or a concept of a biscuit." A troubled student was reported to have said, "I don't know what I've done in the last three years, I reckon I haven't done anything, I haven't any concept." A friend of Wolfe's was also dejected: "I haven't got it. I don't know what I know. I don't know anything." Professor Williams, on the other hand, was rumored to have numerous concepts, most of which he got "under his maple tree."[17]

The most acceptable way to get a concept was to embark upon what Williams called "The Wilderness Experience," in which a man "went to the woods and fought it out." Whether Wolfe undertook such a "Soul wrestling"[18] is not known, but his friend Baxter Columbus Jones, a mountain man and a Primitive Baptist, did. One day, as Wolfe tells it, Jones—"red-haired, gaunt and angular"—came up from Battle Park, an arboreal retreat for initiations and Sunday walks and soul-searching, after an eighteen-hour struggle. Wolfe was crossing the campus as Jones emerged from the forest "like a kangaroo, leaping into the air in intervals, and the first and only words he said were: 'I've had a Concept!' And then he passed—he left me stunned and fastened to an ancient tree, [and] went on down the path, high-bounding, kangaroolike, every step or two, to carry the great news to the host."[19] A secondary method of concept-getting was to talk it out with Williams at his home, always open to student visitors. "Up the path to Horace's house," Wolfe remembered, "—But never about sex —About rather a union with God."[20]

In class Williams enlivened heady philosophic discussions of the concept by inserting down-to-earth examples designed to amuse the students. A favorite illustration was that the concept "of a wheelbarrow is closer to reality than the wheel-barrow itself,"[21] a theory driven home by the question-and-answer method which sometimes went like this: "What is the

When Wolfe first came to the class, Henry Horace Williams, born 1858 in northeastern North Carolina on the edge of the Great Dismal Swamp, was sixty years old. In moneyless times, he managed to graduate from the University of North Carolina and attend Yale and Harvard before returning to Chapel Hill in 1891 as a member of the faculty. He and his wife soon moved to a dilapidated old house in a grove on the outskirts of the village where they kept cows. The house, with no bathtubs or heat, no screens or toilets, was all rather primitive and unsanitary. Increasingly the villagers, especially neighbors of the Williamses, began a series of indignant complaints, grumbling that he was disgusting and miserly, that he mistreated his wife, that the milk from his dairy was unfit to drink. A group from the community was elected to see what could be done about the living conditions of the antediluvian philosopher. Horace's flies became the committee's battlecry. "The barn and the flies," Wolfe jotted down, "—the committee of citizens—He set his price—Finally the barn removed just beyond the stated boundary . . . 'In the Middle Ages [Wolfe reported Williams as saying] vulgar Superstition vented its passion and its cruelty upon the Devil. Men called it religion. More recently vulgar Superstition vents the same passion and the same cruelty against the fly. We call it science —sanitation.' This unfair, but magnificent. Have never heard him speak of the machine—or of the illusion of progress—Yet much more magnificently he was including these things— noble and wholly, as in the Greeks—All great creatures perhaps have in them a touch of magnificent unreason."[28]

The distaste for Horace Williams in the village gradually spread into the state after it was whispered here and there that his philosophy classes were hardly more than vile lessons in atheism. Then, on May 6, 1917, a month after the United States declared war on Germany, Williams said, in a private conversation in Charlotte, that no principle underlay America's involvement in a war between England and Germany, that America winked at the seizure of ships by England, but not by Germany. His comments reached the press, and North Carolina howled with anguish at this pro-German within her borders. Though Williams denied the charge and attempted to defend himself against the false accusation, the patriotic administration at the university was deeply upset. But, wondered Wolfe, "Was not Horace Williams at heart pro German—that is to say Pro-Kant and Pro-Hegel?"[29]

Not only did Williams alienate neighbors at home and North Carolinians far and wide, he also managed to antagonize the faculty. His clearly articulated abhorrence of footnotes and bibliographies kept him at loggerheads with colleagues like Greenlaw, so earnestly committed to the new scientific research methods. "I do not know any great thing that has either foot notes or bibliography," wrote Williams. "Why did St. Paul omit footnotes in the Epistle to the Galatians? It is masterly in every line; but not one foot note and no bibliography. There is not a foot note in the Kritik, nor the Logik." And Williams had no use for specialists: "Of course the Specialist rails at Logic. He says there is nothing in it. For his little specialty that is correct." Economists were blind leaders: "If the Economists can not lead the people along the way that avoids panics, what is their business?"[30] For scientists such as geology professor Collier Cobb, he had an aversion, and they for him: "The indignation of Mr. Collier Cobb—His dislike of Mr. Williams—Dislike of Horace in portions of student body,"[31] Wolfe wrote, remembering how students absorbed the prejudices of favorite professors. Though Williams, strongly garrisoned by the approbation of his "boys," appeared to be unconcerned by these animosities and continued to disparage his colleagues, he was nevertheless stunned in May, 1919, when by secret ballot of the faculty he was not recommended for one of the first endowed Kenan professorships. It was, he said, the "worst blow" he had ever received,[32] presumably unmindful of his constant criticisms of those who at last took their explicable revenge.

Wolfe kept abreast of these village and campus disputes

and, by degrees, as his undivided enchantment with Greenlaw began faintly to ebb, he slipped into the magic circle of
Williams's "boys."

"Mr. W. is a small, wizened man with an enormous, bulbous head, a thin, seamed face and a closely cropped grey
moustache," Wolfe wrote of his professor. "He lectures standing up always with his derby hat on the table before him as
if ready at any moment to make his departure. He measures
the effect of his lecture on the class by the number of times
they look out the window during the hour. If no one looks
out the window Mr. W. will say with great satisfaction at the
end of his lecture: 'I have seldom had a more attentive class
than this one. No one looked out the window to-day'. . . . The
first day I attended my first course under Professor X [Green-
law], he said to us: 'Get the facts. Get the facts and order
them.' The first day I attended the Logic under Mr. W. he
said: 'Gentlemen there's no such thing as a fact.' So there you
are. In philosophy, in modes of thought of study, of regard
for what each considers basical and fundamental each of these
men is the very antithesis of the other. And each is a great
teacher. . . . To an uncanny degree Mr. W. has been able to
stamp himself on the lives of those he has come in contact
with; students are profoundly influenced by him, thru them
he keeps a guiding hand on the affairs of the campus without
appearing to do so. . . . Of late years Mr. W.'s compeers have
dropt off, the 'old school' is about gone, a new, strong, aggres-
sive, scientific, fact-getting group of faculty members have
come in, of whom Professor X is the finest illustration. They
call Mr. W. an old fogy (behind his back, for he's too clever
to argue with—his 'dialectic' confuses them), they say his philosophy is nothing but an old German system of metaphysics,
now outworn and easily to be explained by a newer and more
modern system—psychology. They maintain farther that the
old man leads students on to the primrose path of general-
ization, that he teaches them to sneer at honest, decent grub-

bing, and is therefore a menace and obstacle to good scholarship. . . ."[33]

While Wolfe obviously was aware of the belligerent factions, he jubilantly signed on as a full-time Williams student for the whole of his senior year, taking all three courses in Logic. The class, a "disputatious, questioning crew,"[34] again had a textbook, *The Science of Thought* (1869) by Charles Carroll Everett, Williams's Harvard professor from whom he had appropriated the open-discussion classroom technique.[35] Though Williams followed the text lackadaisically,[36] Wolfe doubtless owned no copy, preferring to dip into Kant and Hegel on his own.[37] The lectures and talk sessions possessed at least a modicum of order. Logic began, Williams proclaimed, with language, and history depended upon the "recovery of a lost language."[38] From then on, knowledge was to be explored through the process of logic. "We were," he said, "as the Skippers of the Clipper ships, each bearing his cargo into port. There was rivalry and enthusiasm [after my lectures]. I recall one day when we had landed after a beautiful sail Mr. Thomas Wolfe from the back seat almost rose in his seat and asked, Where do we go next?"[39]

Often, in order to apply logic to the formulation of a student's moral attitudes, Williams posed such a question as this: What is a fellow to do who is "in love with one girl and engaged to another"?[40] A few in the class thought he ought to marry the girl he loved, others that he ought to honor his engagement, some that he should marry neither, and one concluded humorously that he should move to Utah and marry both.[41] Upon advancing such a puzzler, and while the class sought for an answer, Williams would look out the window and whistle low. If Wolfe came forth with one of his "brilliant flights,"[42] Williams would laugh and away they would go. On those evenings when Wolfe could not bear to postpone submitting some inspired theory he'd had after class or some problem which was on his mind, he would make his way to

Williams's weather-beaten house where he would find the professor sitting with his wife as he prepared his lectures or read Hegel. "Horace a man's man," Wolfe recollected. "She worshipped him—he sent her away calmly as one might a child—His delight in the association of young men—The confessional at evening. He put her out along with the cat."[43]

For the final spring examination, since he had not bothered to take notes, Wolfe borrowed those of his industrious friend William H. Bobbitt, studied them diligently, and got an A on the course, while Bobbitt made only a B. "But then," said Bobbitt, "Horace had already decided that Wolfe was a genius, and no other grade was appropriate."[44]

Meanwhile, Wolfe had digested a sizable abundance of opaque Hegelianism.[45] "The philosophy of negations—Horace's hatred of dualism—In this way he absorbed things in his life—Hegelian Monism does away to a considerable extent with the Yea-and-Nay answer to all things—If it doesn't account for the combined, it accepts it and pretends to understand it—a fascinating system with unending mind-seducing involutions, like Royce's picture of a map with a map, and so on—Why the absolute cannot be apprehended—Truth, Goodness, and Beauty—The Englishmen—Hume, Berkeley, Locke, Spencer—'No time for the little fellows' said he."[46] Williams's lectures, pounding away at the Hegelian dialectic "process of unifying opposites," argued that it was "the nature of action to synthesize, and to exclude the difference." The result of synthesis, in which "Every object is made up of exact opposites,"[47] was a monism embracing differences and discarding dualism. The next step was the forming of a concept, "a Begriff," a blueprint, a "pure knowledge as quality."[48] Besides affirming the principles of Hegelian monism, Williams also preached a Platonic trinitarianism, where truth was exhibited intellectually, goodness actively, and beauty emotionally—a synthesis, Williams contended, which was identical with the tenets of Christianity.[49]

It was all, Wolfe came to realize, "at best a tortuous patched-up scheme. But what was most important was the man himself ... because he supplied to many of us, for the first time in our lives, the inspiration of a questioning intelligence. He taught us not to be afraid to think, to question; to examine critically the most venerable of our native superstitions, our local prejudices, to look hide-bound conventions in the eye and challenge them. In these ways he was a powerful and moving figure." Indeed, the magnetism of the man was so overwhelming that Wolfe and his classmates cared not a whit that their philosopher's "philosophy" was an intricate salmagundi that "came up out of ancient Greece through a great series of 'developments' to Hegel—and *after* Hegel—." Well, after Hegel, "he did not supply the answer, but *after* Hegel was our Old Man."[50]

Williams's decades in Chapel Hill were fortunate ones for him, since his success there would have been impossible in a more sophisticated time and place. "One of the great spirits of the age unfolding quietly in a village," Wolfe wrote. "He had in him a touch of fire—A genius for occasional and conscious malignancy—This is why smaller men ... never really understood him."[51] He did not wish his "boys" to fit into a mold, into a copy of himself. They knew this and revered him for it. If some of them delighted in his nebulous, abstruse discussions, and if at times others, like Wolfe, were entertained by the showmanship of the Old Man, all of them were always aware that his highest justification was that they simply be no one but themselves.

Can one doubt that on that last evening in Chapel Hill Wolfe sought out Williams, honoring his final commission to himself?

On the following hot June morning, one can see Wolfe, after hurriedly packing papers and books and clothes, walking to C. S. Pendergraft's stand and buying a seat in the jitney for Durham and the Asheville train. As the jitney moved down Franklin Street under the arch of the summer trees, he heard the "ringing of the great bell" and then, leaving the old campus behind and ascending a gentle rise to the crest of the hill before plunging to the flatlands, Wolfe turned his eyes to the left toward a grove and the house beyond, and there he saw, as though waiting for him, as though the now swiftly fading magic might return for one moment more, "Horace at his window." [52]

Wolfe, age 16 (Wolfe family album, U.N.C. Library).

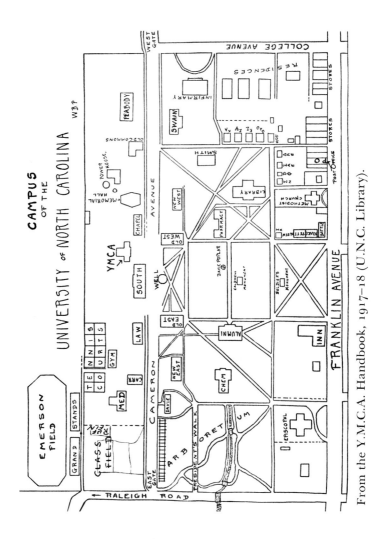

From the Y.M.C.A. Handbook, 1917–18 (U.N.C. Library).

The north side of Franklin Street about 1919 (N.C. Collection, U.N.C. Library).

Interior of the Pickwick Theater (N.C. Collection, U.N.C. Library).

"Shorty" Spruill, Nat Mobley, Wolfe, Jeff Bynum—Pi Kappa Phis after Golden Fleece initiation, May 1919 (Jefferson C. Bynum's Photo Album, U.N.C. Library).

Paul Green, about 1920 (U.N.C. Library).

Two unidentified friends, Wolfe, John S. Terry, about 1918
(Jefferson C. Bynum's Photo Album, U.N.C. Library).

Jonathan Daniels, Frederick J. Cohn, and Wolfe in
"The Third Night" (*Yackety Yack* 1920).

Above: Edwin A. Greenlaw
(N.C. Collection,
U.N.C. Library).

Left: William Stanly Bernard
(U.N.C. Photo Laboratory).

Right: Frederick H. Koch, 1918
(U.N.C. Library).

Below: Henry Horace Williams
(Sam Hood).

JOHN SKALLY TERRY
ROCKINGHAM, N. C.
Age, 25; Weight, 270; Height, 5 feet 9¼ inches

A.B., '18; Permanent President Class of '18; Secretary-Treasurer Class (2), Treasurer (3), Vice-President (4); Di Society, President (4), Vice-President (3); Greater Council (4); Assistant in Zoology (3); Assistant Editor-in-Chief *Magazine* (4); Assistant Editor *Tar Heel* (4, 5); Associate Editor YACKETY YACK (4); Advisory Editor *Tar Baby* (6); Latin-American Club; International Polity Club; Senior Stunt Committee; Medical Society; Y. M. C. A. Cabinet (5); Chairman Health Reconstruction Committee North Caroline Club (6); Honors in Language and Literature.

Σ Υ; Ω Δ; Ε Φ Δ; Φ Χ; Φ Β Κ.

THE Class of '18 has priority of claim upon John, but it is during the routine of his subsequent years in medicine that we have come to know him best. In addition to his scientific tendency he possesses a splendid natural literary ability, which we believe he will not permit to atrophy. We look upon him as our logical representative in the field of medical literature, and would not be surprised if—like Holmes—he should some day produce a work which will rank as a classic.

THOMAS CLAYTON WOLFE
ASHEVILLE, N. C.
Age, 19; Weight, 178; Height, 6 feet 3 inches

Di Society; Buncombe County Club; Freshman-Sophomore Debate (2); Dramatic Association; Carolina Playmakers (3, 4), Author two One-Act Plays, Executive Committee (4); Associate Editor YACKETY YACK (3); Associate Editor *Magazine* (3), Assistant Editor-in-Chief (4); Managing Editor *Tar Heel* (3), Editor-in-Chief (4); Advisory Board *Tar Baby* (4); Worth Prize in Philosophy (3); Y. M. C. A. Cabinet (3, 4); Student Council (4); Athletic Council (4); Class Poet (3, 4); Chairman Junior Stunt Committee; German Club; Amphoterothen; Satyrs; Golden Fleece.

Σ Υ; Ω Δ; Π Κ Φ.

EDITING the *Tar Heel*, winning Horace's philosophy prize when only a Junior, writing plays and then showing the world how they should be acted—they are all alike to this young Shakespeare. Last year he played the leading role in the "Midnight Frolic" at "Gooch's Winter Palace", but this year it's the leading role on the "Carolina Shipping Board". But, seriously speaking, "Buck" is a great, big fellow. He can do more between 8:25 and 8:30 than the rest of us can do all day, and it is no wonder that he is classed as a genius.

One Hundred Three

Yearbook entries for Wolfe and John S. Terry from *Yackety Yack,* 1920.

Appendix

Dramatic Fragment about Horace Williams

From time to time, especially during the three years after Wolfe left Chapel Hill, the personality of Horace Williams tugged at his creative imagination. Among his unpublished manuscripts are a number of fragments based on Williams, each one presumably the first step for a play about the man. They range from a one-page conversation[1] to an outline of twenty-two pages for a full-length play.[2] Some of the fragments are in dramatic form, others provide a prose synopsis with suggested dialogue, one is little more than a cast of characters,[3] and another, excerpts from which were used in the last chapter of this book,[4] is simply factual biography.

Williams's home life is portrayed in two fragments,[5] his fancied illness, death, and its aftermath in four others.[6] At least five introduce students or former students,[7] and the conflict between Williams (called variously Bagget or Wilson, but generally Tasker Weldon) and other faculty members is subject of seven.[8] At one point, Wolfe toyed with the notion of a prose narrative about Williams, then quickly switched to a Job-like dramatic account in which Satan appears declaiming in iambic pentameters.[9]

Wolfe, in various guises, is often among the cast of characters. One of the fragments has a professor and a lawyer discussing the posthumous publication of Professor Weldon's diary, described as "a revelation," "passionate" and "personal." The lawyer reads aloud an excerpt from it: "Mr. Reed [Wolfe] has an electric current passing through him. He watches me like a hawk when I lecture and when he asks a question he never fails to lean forward in his seat and bend toward me. What brilliant eyes he has! . . . I must watch Reed. One of his questions almost had me in a corner today. The man bears watching. . . . I intend to give Reed grade *A*. . . ." [10]

Toward the last of his three-year study at Harvard, Wolfe sent the first acts of six different plays to his drama professor, George Pierce Baker, for inspection, one of them a dialogue between a book-devouring student named Ramsay and Professor Wilson, his teacher of philosophy. [11] An untitled dramatic fragment, [12] presumably an early version of the first act of this play, might be called

Ramsay and the Philosopher

Scene: The library in the home of Professor Wilson. It is a huge, oak-panelled room covered on three sides by bookshelves, the only interstices being for double windows at the back and doors in the right and left walls. It is a philosopher's library; these shelves hold no plays or novels. There is a long table in the center of the room. It is littered with books and papers for the philosopher studies the daily news as carefully as he reads a well-cherished book—say, "Die Phenomenologie des Geistes" of Hegel. On the tops of the book-shelves are placed several marble busts of the Greek philosophers.

There are engravings of the ruins at Athens and a picture of Martin Luther, "the son of a blacksmith," the philosopher's supreme example of character, standing across a table from the combined power of Europe. The picture represents the occasion when Luther said: "Ich kann nicht anders."

It is a warm, moonlit night in early summer. The windows at the back disclose the opulence of a Southern scene. One looks across an elm-shaded street into the depths of a cavern of green, the college campus. Moonlight rains down through the trees and makes mysterious little glooms and lights on the campus and on the old buildings, some of which are visible. The campus sweeps gradually up to a gentle knoll where there is a college well covered by a round top supported by white Corinthian columns. A soft breeze puffs at the heavy window hangings.

The room is at first empty but from the door at the left comes the sound of voices, laughter, occasional applause, and the racket of knives and forks. Professor Wilson is giving a farewell spread to the elect of his class in the Logic. Finally there is a furious burst of applause, followed by the scraping of chairs and Wilson enters the room accompanied by six young men. They are all in high spirits, their laughter and badinage mingling pleasantly with the professor's husky chuckle.

Professor Wilson is a man in the middle sixties. His figure is slight, but strong and active, his thin, seamed face is colored by a ruddy glow. But one notices immediately the head. The forehead is high and enormously wide; the contour of the head is bulbous; it dominates his slight figure like a large flame a small candle. Penetrating grey eyes are sunk deep into their tired, brown sockets.

Wilson (opening a box of cigars on the table): Here are cigars. You can throw out the smoke screen when you are ready. (They help themselves.)

A Student: Watch Hegel, Professor. He took a half dozen.

Wilson: And who's Hegel, Mr. Todd?

Student (pointing to a young man at the table): It's a new name I've given him since he got A on your course.

Wilson: Did you hear that, Mr. Ramsay?

Ramsay: In one ear and out another, Professor. I have no time for these schoolboy jokes—since I made an A on Logic.

Todd: You don't give many A's, do you, Professor?

Wilson: No. I'm very stingy with them. I've given three in thirty years. Mr. Ramsay was the last.

Todd: Who were the other two?

(All listen with interest.)

Wilson: I won't tell you their names. One [Edward Kidder Graham] went out and became a very great man. He was made president of a university when he was thirty-five. He was a very great man—in mind and spirit.

Todd: Yes, I know who you mean.

Wilson: Then he made a mistake; sometimes I think the greatest mistake in nineteen hundred years. He died.

Todd: Say,—that *is* a mistake, isn't it? What became of the other one?

Wilson (laughing): Oh, you want to know too much, Mr. Todd.

Several (at once): Oh, come on and tell us, Professor.

Wilson: Well, he went out and became a real-estate man,— and a very successful one too. (With a dry chuckle.) Now, gentlemen, if you ever want to do me a good turn, get hold of a young man who is coming here to enter the school of Commerce and tell him that "Wee Willie" Wilson—for I believe that's the name you have given me—tell him that Wee Willie turns out not only good college presidents but good real-estate men, and if he wants a practical education to take my Logic.

Several: Amen!

Wilson: And that reminds me: If you know any ministerial students— (He is interrupted by laughter.) Yes, I mean that too. Let me have a boy for two years before he enters the theological school and I'll teach him to think. After that, they can't touch him. (Applause and cries of "Speech.") No; I think not. It seems to me I must have made a half dozen speeches tonight.

Todd: Just a few words of farewell, Professor.

Wilson: Very well. Perhaps there is something I might say to you now. Come over here with me under this picture. (They all

[Page or pages missing]

Ramsay: That won't affect Todd, Professor. He has a girl in every port. He's our Passionate Pilgrim.

Wilson: Is that so? Then I have a word for you, Mr. Todd: Keep away from red-haired women. (This breaks up the meeting. They come forward, one by one, to bid him goodbye.)

Travis (small, fat, good-humored): This is the last chance I'll have to see you before I go, Professor.

Wilson: You are taking that position with the bank?

Travis: Yes, sir.

Wilson: Good. I think it was a wise decision. (Confidentially.) I have often wondered why the human spirit expresses itself through the trust. Think that over and write me about it. Goodbye, Mr. Travis.

Travis: Goodbye, sir. (He goes out.)

Joyce (rawboned, strong, ponderous): Well, goodbye, Professor. I'm leaving tomorrow.

Wilson: What are your plans, Mr. Joyce?

Joyce: I'm going into father's mill. From the ground up.

Wilson (approvingly): Good. (In low tones.) You will come into contact with the most perplexing problem before the nation today—that of industry. I hope you'll study it carefully and let me have your opinion. I'm very much interested.

Joyce (heartily): I will, sir. Goodbye, Professor. (They grasp hands and he goes.)

Graham (tall, slight, energetic): I've had a great evening, Professor.

Wilson: When are you leaving, Mr. Graham?

Graham: Tomorrow. I'll not see you again before I go. I may be back through during the summer. Will you be here?

Wilson: Yes. Come around and see the old man. What are your plans?

Graham: I'm going to Europe for a year. Then I'll return and go into business with father. Goodbye, sir. (He goes.)

(Two others say their goodbyes and go. Ramsay is left.)

Ramsay: Goodbye, Professor. I've had a very pleasant evening.

Wilson (consulting his watch): Ten o'clock. Are you in a hurry?

Ramsay: Why—no.

Wilson: Sit down and stay a while. I want to talk to you. (They find chairs and are silent a moment.) Well, what have you decided to do?

Ramsay: I'm going to that newspaper.

Wilson (after a slight pause): You have thought it over carefully.

Ramsay: Yes, sir.

Wilson: Then, you know best. (A pause.) You'd make a great teacher, Mr. Ramsay.

Ramsay: Do you think so? I'm afraid I haven't the proper temperament, Professor.

Wilson: Judging you by most of my associates, you haven't. But you have what is most needed. I've brought you to the point where they can't touch your fire and spirit now. I give myself full credit for that. And you have it in you to set other minds on fire. That is a rare quality.

Ramsay: Thank you. I hope you're right. I've thought the matter over carefully. When I said temperament, I meant scholarly temperament. By that I mean the ability to be painstaking and thorough within limits, within narrow limits. But I can't limit myself that way.

[Last half of page blank].

Wilson: Have you a girl?

Ramsay: No, sir.

Wilson: Good. You don't want one.

Ramsay: But you said to the others—

Wilson (waving his hand): Never mind that. I'm talking to you now. You don't want one.

Ramsay (with a grin): Well, I wouldn't say that, Professor. You know I'm human like the rest of them.

[Breaks off. Two additional pages, not closely connected with the foregoing, seem to be from a synopsis of the action Wolfe planned for further developing the play.]

My acknowledgment of the diligent efforts of Don Bishop and John S. Terry, both of whom were assiduous in gathering reminiscences of Wolfe as a student at the University of North Carolina when his contemporaries were available and memories were fresh, is abundantly and gratefully evinced throughout the notes which follow. Two antecedent studies based almost entirely on printed sources—Agatha Boyd Adams, *Thomas Wolfe: Carolina Student* (Chapel Hill: University of North Carolina Library, 1950), and Robert Coleman Gibbs, "Thomas Wolfe's Four Years at Chapel Hill: A Study of Biographical Source Material," Thesis, University of North Carolina, 1958—were primarily useful as indicators. In the notes I have attempted, whenever possible and not inappropriate, to cite manuscript and first printed sources only—not subsequent, often multiple, use of the sources.

I have had correspondence and interviews with LeGette Blythe, William H. Bobbitt, Albert and Gladys Coates, Frederick J. Cohn, Ben Cone, Sr., Jonathan Daniels, Watt W. Eagle, Sam J. Ervin, Jr., Paul and Elizabeth Green, Charles M. Hazlehurst, Robert B. House, James S. Howell, Parkhill O. Jarvis, J. Y. Jordan, Jr., Dewey (Mrs. Lawrence) London, Dougald MacMillan, Fred Moore, John Burke O'Donnell, Moses Rountree, Corydon P. and Julia Spruill, Charles G. Tennent, George Raby Tennent, Francis Dubose Uzzell, Fred Wolfe, and Richard L. Young, and to all I hereby express my gratitude. Guy Owen, Manly Wade

Wellman, and Mrs. Allen G. Gill provided me with valuable information, as did Nathan G. Gooding.

Abbreviations for sources and locations frequently appearing in the notes are:

AO   Autobiographical Outline, bMS Am 1883 (191), begun in July, 1926, after Wolfe's decision to write a novel. (See *Notebooks*, I, xxxi, 60.) A series of phrases containing experiences and impressions, in two notebooks. In the second notebook, the first 56 unnumbered pages (but numbered in the notes below for citation purposes) cover the years 1916–20.

bMS Am 1883   The Thomas Wolfe Collection of William B. Wisdom, Harvard College Library. Manuscripts and Wolfe's personal library.

Car. Mag.   *Carolina Magazine*, student literary journal at the University of North Carolina, has several slightly varying titles.

Directory   *Directory Faculty and Students of the University of North Carolina*, 1916–17, 1917–18, Jan.-June 1919, 1919–20.

Letters   *The Letters of Thomas Wolfe*, ed. Elizabeth Nowell. New York: Scribner's, 1956.

NcU   The Library, University of North Carolina at Chapel Hill.

Notebooks   *The Notebooks of Thomas Wolfe*, ed. Richard S. Kennedy and Paschal Reeves. 2 vols. Chapel Hill: Univ. of North Carolina Press, 1970.

TH   *The Tar Heel*, 1916–20, student weekly newspaper at the University of North Carolina.

TW-NcU   The Thomas Wolfe Collection in the Library of the University of North Carolina at Chapel Hill, containing 82 boxes of manuscripts and other material donated by the Wolfe family, the John S. Terry estate, Don Bishop, and others. Only a portion of the collection has been catalogued.

U.N.C.   University of North Carolina at Chapel Hill.

YY   *Yackety Yack*, student yearbook, U.N.C.

1. Freshman

1. Hayden Norwood, *The Marble Man's Wife: Thomas Wolfe's Mother* (New York: Scribner's, 1947), p. 168.

2. *Asheville Gazette-News*, Apr. 12, 1913.

3. John S. Terry, notes, TW-NcU.   5. *Asheville Citizen*, June 1, 1916.

4. *Notebooks*, I, 3.   6. *Asheville Citizen*, June 2, 1916.

7. AO, p. 47.   8. TW-NcU.

9. Frank A. Dixon, in *Independent* (Anderson, S. C.), July 31, 1948.

10. Mabel Wolfe Wheaton, with LeGette Blythe, *Thomas Wolfe and His Family* (Garden City, N. Y.: Doubleday, 1961), p. 138.

11. Ed Yoder, in *TH*, Nov. 1, 1953.

12. Elizabeth Nowell, *Thomas Wolfe* (Garden City, N. Y.: Doubleday, 1960), p. 33.

13. Mrs. Julia W. Wolfe, " 'Eliza Gant' Talks," manuscript transcription by Ruth Davis, n.d., p. 6, TW-NcU.

14. Mabel Wolfe Wheaton to Fred Wolfe, [Aug. 8, 1916], TW-NcU.

15. Wolfe to Ralph Wheaton, Aug. 18, 1916, TW-NcU.

16. Andrew Turnbull, *Thomas Wolfe* (New York: Scribner's, 1967), p. 18.

17. Wheaton, p. 161.   18. *Letters*, p. 3.

19. W. O. Wolfe to Ralph Wheaton, Sept. 9, 1916, TW-NcU.

20. *TH*, Sept. 15, 1916.

21. Charles M. Hazlehurst, interview, Nov. 27, 1973.

22. AO, p. 1.   28. *TH*, Sept. 15, 1916.

23. Later the site of Hillel house.   29. *TH*, Feb. 10, 1917.

24. *Letters*, p. 3.   30. AO, p. 1.

25. *Directory*, 1916–17.   31. *YY*, 1917, p. 36.

26. *TH*, Sept. 23, 1916.   32. AO, p. 2.

27. *Directory*, 1916–17, 1917–18.   33. Turnbull, p. 23.

34. Richard S. Kennedy, *The Window of Memory: The Literary Career of Thomas Wolfe* (Chapel Hill: Univ. of North Carolina Press, 1962), p. 40.

35. *Asheville Citizen-Times*, Nov. 19, 1950.

36. U.N.C. *Catalogue, 1916–17*, p. 73.

37. Turnbull, p. 23.

38. Floyd C. Watkins, *Thomas Wolfe's Characters* (Norman: Univ. of Oklahoma Press, 1957), pp. 17–18.

39. John O. Lyons, *The College Novel in America* (Carbondale: Southern Illinois Univ. Press, 1962), p. 78.

40. U.N.C. *Catalogue*, 1916–17, p. 141.

41. Ben Cone, Sr., interview, Sept. 17, 1974.

42. "Notes on Professor John S. Terry's Address to the Book Club of Washington Square College, New York University," typescript, TW-NcU.

43. Robert Watson Winston, *Horace Williams: Gadfly of Chapel Hill* (Chapel Hill: Univ. of North Carolina Press, 1942), pp. 129–30.

44. Dialectic Society minutes, Sept. 23, 1916, Southern Historical Collection, NcU.

45. Don Bishop, in *Greensboro Daily News*, Sept. 28, 1947.

46. *Letters*, pp. 3–4, where Wolfe's letter to his brother is inaccurately transcribed. See the mutilated original, TW-NcU.

47. Watt W. Eagle, interview, July 28, 1971.

48. Sam J. Ervin, Jr., interview, Sept. 14, 1971.

49. *TH*, Oct. 7, 1916.

50. *TH*, Oct. 14, 1916.   51. *TH*, Oct. 28, 1916.

52. W. O. Wolfe to Fred Wolfe, Oct. 3, 1916, TW-NcU.

53. Charles G. Tennent to John S. Terry, Apr. 24, 1944, TW-NcU.

54. According to George Raby Tennent, as reported to Manly Wade Wellman, interview, Oct. 4, 1974.

55. Richard L. Young, interview, June 17, 1974.

56. Louis R. Wilson, *The University of North Carolina, 1900–1930* (Chapel Hill: Univ. of North Carolina Press, 1964), p. 253.

57. Watt W. Eagle, interview, July 28, 1971.

58. bMS Am 1883 (1261)

59. Dialectic Society minutes, Nov. 4, Dec. 9, 1916.

60. AO, p. 1.

61. According to Lena Mae Williams, as reported by Gladys Coates, interview, Dec. 4, 1973.

62. bMS Am 1883 (1307), folder 6.

63. Ben Cone, Sr., interview, Sept. 17, 1974.

64. According to Francis F. Bradshaw, Don Bishop notes, TW-NcU.

65. "New Wolfe Book May Be Published," *News and Observer* (Raleigh), Feb. 12, 1948, where street number is incorrectly given as 524.

66. John Burke O'Donnell, interview, Aug. 4, 1976.

67. *TH*, Nov. 25, 1916; *Notebooks*, II, 924.

68. *TH*, Dec. 2, 1916.   69. *TH*, Dec. 9, 1916.

70. *TH*, Dec. 13, 1919. See Richard Walser, "An Early Wolfe Essay—and the Downfall of a Hero," *Modern Fiction Studies*, 11 (1965), 269–74, where the essay is reprinted.

71. AO, p. 2.   74. AO, p. 2.

72. *Notebooks*, II, 736.   75. U.N.C. Records office.

73. AO, p. 2.   76. *TH*, Feb. 10, 1917.

77. Paul Green, interview, Apr. 18, 1975.

78. AO, p. 2; George Raby Tennent to Richard Walser, Apr. 12, 1975, and James S. Howell, Aug. 27, 1975.

79. Wheaton, p. 247.

80. Robert B. House, *The Light That Shines: Chapel Hill, 1912–1916* (Chapel Hill: Univ. of North Carolina Press, 1964), p. 34.

81. James S. Howell to Richard Walser, Aug. 27, 1975.

82. *TH*, Feb. 10, 1917.

83. Dialectic Society minutes, Feb. 24, 1917.

84. On handwritten rough draft of Registration Blank for Harvard University Appointment Office, TW-NcU.

85. *YY*, 1918, p. 61.

86. LeGette Blythe, in *Charlotte Observer*, May 9, 1943.

87. LeGette Blythe to John S. Terry, undated [spring 1943?], TW-NcU.

88. *Notebooks*, II, 854.

89. *YY*, 1920, p. 177.   90. AO, p. 9; *Notebooks*, I, 133.

91. Thomas Wolfe, "Chapel Hill Recollections," ca. 1932, bMS Am 1883 (1172).

92. AO, p. 53.   93. Wilson, p. 263.

94. *TH*, Mar. 24, 1917.   95. Wilson, p. 263.

96. Don Bishop, "Thomas Wolfe," *Car. Mag.*, Mar. 1942, p. 35.

97. *TH*, Oct. 14, 1916.   99. *Letters*, p. 193.

98. *TH*, Mar. 24, 1917.   100. AO, p. 1.

101. Pocahontas Wight Edmunds, *Tar Heels Track the Century* (Raleigh: Edwards & Broughton, 1966), p. 267.

102. Wheaton, p. 165.   103. AO, p. 2.

104. Don Bishop, "Thomas Wolfe," *Car. Mag.*, Mar. 1942, p. 35.

105. "Transcription of Recorded Interviews between Julia E. Wolfe and John S. Terry," p. 5, TW-NcU.

106. Edmunds, p. 268.   107. AO, p. 2.

108. Paul Green, interview, July 18, 1968.

109. *TH*, Apr. 28, 1917.

110. *TH*, May 5, 1917.   111. *Notebooks*, I, 80.

2. Bully Bernard

1. Clement Eaton, "Student Days with Thomas Wolfe," *Georgia Review*, 17 (1963), 149.

2. AO, p. 33.

3. *Alumni History of the University of North Carolina*, 2nd ed. (Chapel Hill: General Alumni Association, 1924), p. 48.

4. Robert B. House, *The Light That Shines: Chapel Hill, 1912–1916* (Chapel Hill: Univ. of North Carolina Press, 1964), p. 184.

5. U.N.C. *Catalogue, 1916–17*, p. 69.

6. Benjamin H. Wolfe to Wolfe, Feb. 19, 1917, TW-NcU.

7. *Notebooks*, I, 80.

8. Dewey (Mrs. Lawrence) London, interview, Nov. 14, 1973.

9. AO, p. 33.

10. *YY*, 1919, p. 340.

11. Andrew Turnbull, *Thomas Wolfe* (New York: Scribner's, 1967), p. 26.

12. Alden Stahr, "Thomas Wolfe at Chapel Hill," *Car. Mag.*, Apr. 24, 1932, p. 1.

13. Wolfe to Albert Coates, ca. 1921, photocopy, TW-NcU.

14. Turnbull, p. 26.

15. Richard S. Kennedy, in Paschal Reeves, ed., *Thomas Wolfe and the Glass of Time* (Athens: Univ. of Georgia Press, 1971), p. 74.

16. Stahr, p. 1.

17. Forrest G. Miles to Don Bishop, Jan. 16, 1941, typescript copy, TW-NcU.

18. *Letters*, p. 343.

19. Henry T. Volkening, "Thomas Wolfe: Penance No More," in Thomas Clark Pollock and Oscar Cargill, *Thomas Wolfe at Washington Square* (New York: New York Univ. Press, 1954), p. 119.

20. Quoted by Turnbull, p. 27.

3. Sophomore

1. Wolfe to Benjamin H. Wolfe, July 11, 1917, TW-NcU.

2. *Letters*, p. 4.

3. W. O. Wolfe to Benjamin H. Wolfe, July 9, 1917, typescript copy, TW-NcU.

4. Mabel Wolfe Wheaton, with LeGette Blythe, *Thomas Wolfe and His Family* (Garden City, N. Y.: Doubleday, 1961), p. 156.

5. W. O. Wolfe to Benjamin H. Wolfe, July 23, 1917, TW-NcU.

6. AO, pp. 5–6.

7. AO, p. 3.   8. AO, p. 5.

9. According to Guy Owen, as reported by residents of Anderson, Nov. 18, 1974.

10. *Letters*, p. 66.

11. Elizabeth Nowell, *Thomas Wolfe* (Garden City, N. Y.: Doubleday, 1960), p. 35.

12. Hayden Norwood, *The Marble Man's Wife: Thomas Wolfe's Mother* (New York: Scribner's, 1947), p. 34.

13. Ethel Ryan, "Thomas Wolfe Kept One Secret," *News and Observer* (Raleigh), Sept. 26, 1965.

14. AO, p. 3.   15. *Letters*, p. 5.

16. Louis R. Wilson, *The University of North Carolina, 1900–1930* (Chapel Hill: Univ. of North Carolina Press, 1957), p. 265.

17. *YY*, 1918, p. 178.

18. Thomas Wolfe, "Chapel Hill Recollections," ca. 1932, bMS Am 1883 (1172).

19. *TH*, Oct. 13, 1917.   20. John S. Terry, notes, TW-NcU.

21. J. Y. Jordan, Jr., to Don Bishop, Mar. 5, 1942, typescript copy, TW-NcU.

22. Frederick J. Cohn, interview, July 2, 1974.

23. U.N.C. *Catalogue, 1916–17*, p. 73.   25. Nov. 1, 1917, TW-NcU.

24. bMS AM 1883.   26. *TH*, Oct. 6, 1917.

27. William H. Bobbitt, interview, Dec. 7, 1973.

28. Thomas Wolfe, *The Story of a Novel* (New York: Scribner's, 1936), p. 5.

29. Don Bishop, in *Asheville Citizen*, May 25, 1947.

30. W. O. Wolfe to Wolfe, Nov. 21, 1917, TW-NcU.

31. The poem is mentioned in *Thomas Wolfe's Purdue Speech "Writing and Living,"* ed. William Braswell and Leslie A. Field ([West Lafayette, Ind.]: Purdue Univ. Studies, 1964), p. 36.

32. Earl Harris, "Chapel Hill—What It Is," *Car. Mag.*, Apr. 1917, pp. 250–54.

33. AO, p. 7.   34. *TH*, Mar. 16, 1918.

35. *Car. Mag.*, May 1917, pp. 335–36.

36. Pete Ivey, "Tommy Wolfe's School Days," *State* (Raleigh), May 25, 1935, p. 9.

37. According to W. H. Andrews, Jr., Don Bishop notes, TW-NcU.

38. Charles M. Hazlehurst, interview, Nov. 27, 1973.

39. Charles Angoff, "A Promise and a Legend," *North American Review*, 248 (Autumn 1939), 198–201, reprinted in *Thomas Wolfe: The Critical Reception*, ed. Paschal Reeves (New York: David Lewis, 1974), p. 132.

40. Richard L. Young, interview, June 17, 1974.

41. John [John Lee Aycock?] to John S. Terry, Feb. 27, 1947, TW-NcU.

42. Don Bishop, "Thomas Wolfe," *Car. Mag.*, Mar. 1942, p. 35.

43. *The Letters of Thomas Wolfe to His Mother*, ed. C. Hugh Holman and Sue Fields Ross (Chapel Hill: Univ. of North Carolina Press, 1968), p. 4.

44. Forrest G. Miles to Don Bishop, Jan. 16, 1941, typescript copy, TW-NcU.

45. Quoted by Lewis W. Green, in *Asheville Citizen-Times*, Aug. 2, 1964.

46. According to George Denny, as reported by Bennett Cerf, *Saturday Review of Literature*, May 28, 1949, pp. 6–7.

47. *Letters*, p. 6.

48. W. O. Wolfe to Wolfe, Oct. 6, 1917, typescript copy, TW-NcU.

49. *The Letters of Thomas Wolfe to His Mother*, p. 4.

50. W. O. Wolfe to Wolfe, Nov. 21, 1917, TW-NcU.

51. *Letters*, p. 156.

52. Diary (1918) of Ellen Lay, younger sister of Elizabeth Lay (Mrs. Paul) Green, who owns a typescript copy of the diary.

53. *Car. Mag.*, Mar. 1918, p. 294.   54. AO, p. 7.

55. Mrs. Eric A. Abernethy, Don Bishop notes, TW-NcU.

56. TH, Apr. 13, 1918.

57. Dialectic Society minutes, Nov. 30, 1917, Feb. 15, Mar. 30, Apr. 19, 1918, Southern Historical Collection, NcU.

58. C. Hugh Holman, *The Loneliness at the Core: Studies in Thomas Wolfe* (Baton Rouge: Louisiana State Univ. Press, 1975), p. 86.

59. bMS Am 1883 (1262).

60. *TH*, Mar. 23, May 11, 1918; "Debates and Orations in 1918," *YY*, 1919, unnumbered page.

61. Dialectic Society minutes, May 11, 1918.

62. Don Bishop, "Thomas Wolfe," p. 47.

63. *Purdue Speech*, p. 36.   64. *TH*, Mar. 23, 1918.

65. *Purdue Speech*, pp. 35–36. See also Thomas Wolfe, *You Can't Go Home Again* (New York: Harper, 1940), pp. 710–11.

66. Ed Wallace, in *New York World-Telegram*, May 16, 1947.

67. *TH*, Mar. 23, 1918.

68. *Asheville Citizen*, Apr. 5, 1918.

69. W. O. Wolfe to Wolfe, Apr. 17, 1918, typescript copy, TW-NcU.

70. *The Letters of Thomas Wolfe to His Mother*, p. 5.

71. AO, p. 5.

72. *Letters*, p. 6.   73. AO, p. 8.

74. Thomas Wolfe, "Chapel Hill Recollections."

75. George Raby Tennent to Richard Walser, Apr. 12, 1975.

76. Charles M. Hazlehurst, interview, Nov. 27, 1973.

77. Jonathan Daniels, *Thomas Wolfe: October Recollections* (Columbia, S. C.: Bostic & Thornley, 1961), p. 11.

78. J. Y. Jordan, Jr., to John S. Terry, Sept. 25, 1951, TW-NcU.

79. Quoted by Don Bishop, in *Asheville Citizen*, May 25, 1947.

80. Richard L. Young, interview, June 17, 1974.

81. Richard L. Young, in James A. Davis, "The Enigma of Thomas Wolfe," WBT Radio (Charlotte) Project Sixty, May 12, 1961.

82. AO, p. 8.   83. *Letters*, p. 7.

84. Corydon P. Spruill, interview, Nov. 14, 1973.

85. Benjamin H. Wolfe to Mrs. Julia W. Wolfe, Apr. 4, 1918, TW-NcU.

86. AO, p. 22.

87. Benjamin H. Wolfe to Mrs. Julia W. Wolfe, Apr. 4, 1918, TW-NcU.

88. *TH*, Mar. 30, 1918.

89. W. O. Wolfe to Wolfe, Apr. 4, 1918, TW-NcU.

90. *YY*, 1920, p. 49.

91. *TH*, Mar. 30, 1918.

92. Donnell Van Noppen to Don Bishop, Feb. 6, 1941, typescript copy, TW-NcU.

93. LeGette Blythe, "The Thomas Wolfe I Knew," *Charlotte Observer*, Oct. 14, 1945.

94. Hilton G. West to John S. Terry, Mar. 19, 1947, TW-NcU.

95. Moses Rountree to Richard Walser, Dec. 4, 1974.

96. *TH*, Dec. 20, 1918.

97. *TH*, Mar. 30, 1918.

98. Andrew Turnbull, *Thomas Wolfe* (New York: Scribner's, 1967), p. 27.

99. AO, pp. 5–6. See *The Complete Poetical Works of Samuel Taylor Coleridge*, ed. Ernest Hartley Coleridge (Oxford: Clarendon Press, 1912), I, 146–47; E. K. Chambers, *Samuel Taylor Coleridge: A Biographical Study* (Oxford: Clarendon Press, 1938), p. 18; and Wylie Sypher, *Guinea's Captive Kings* (New York: Octagon Books, 1969), p. 217.

100. J. Y. Jordan, Jr., to Don Bishop, Mar. 5, 1942, typescript copy, TW-NcU.

101. Quoted by Marjorie Hunter, in *Journal and Sentinel* (Winston-Salem), July 3, 1955.

102. Nathan Mobley, Don Bishop notes, TW-NcU.

103. *TH*, May 11, 1918; Y.M.C.A. *Handbook of the University of North Carolina, 1918–1919*, p. 36; Agatha Boyd Adams, *Thomas Wolfe: Carolina Student* (Chapel Hill: Univ. of North Carolina Library, 1950), p. 31.

104. *TH*, Apr. 27, 1918.

105. *TH*, May 22, 1918.

106. AO, p. 10.

107. AO, p. 7.

108. Confidential source.

109. All letters in either typescript copy or manuscript, TW-NcU.

110. W. O. Wolfe to Benjamin H. Wolfe, May 1, 1918, TW-NcU.

111. Norwood, p. 63.

4. Edwin Greenlaw

1. *Letters*, p. 16.
2. Richard S. Kennedy, *The Window of Memory: The Literary Career of Thomas Wolfe* (Chapel Hill: Univ. of North Carolina Press, 1962), p. 39.
3. Clement Eaton, "Student Days with Thomas Wolfe," *Georgia Review*, 17 (1963), 147.
4. Dougald MacMillan, *English at Chapel Hill, 1795–1969* (Chapel Hill: Department of English, U.N.C., [1970]), p. 45.
5. bMS Am 1883 (54).
6. U.N.C. *Catalogue, 1916–1917*, p. 61.
7. Among the Wolfe family papers, TW-NcU.
8. Frank O. Ray to John S. Terry, May 12, 1943. TW-NcU.
9. AO, p. 10.
10. Andrew Turnbull, *Thomas Wolfe* (New York: Scribner's, 1967), p. 31.
11. Foreword, *The Blue Ridge Magazine* (NcU), "Published by English 21," Apr. 1920.
12. Garland Burns Porter to Wolfe, Feb. 14, 1937, bMS Am 1883.1 (525).
13. LeGette Blythe, interview, Apr. 19, 1973.
14. Forrest G. Miles to Don Bishop, Jan. 16, 1941, typescript copy, TW-NcU.
15. John [John Lee Aycock?] to John S. Terry, Feb. 27, 1947, TW-NcU.
16. Donnell Van Noppen to Don Bishop, Feb. 6, 1941, typescript copy, TW-NcU.
17. James Mandel, "Thomas Wolfe: A Reminisence [*sic*]," in Thomas Clark Pollock and Oscar Cargill, *Thomas Wolfe at Washington Square* (New York: New York Univ. Press, 1954), p. 99.
18. E. Earle Rives to Don Bishop, Feb. 14, 1941, typescript copy, TW-NcU; William Carmichael, tape (NcU) of Wolfe reminiscences at a dinner, Chapel Hill, Dec. 5, 1958.
19. LeGette Blythe, "About Tom Wolfe," in *The Miscellany* (Davidson College), Dec. 1966, p. 47.
20. Don Bishop, "Thomas Wolfe," *Car. Mag.*, Mar. 1942, p. 47
21. Foreword, *The Peace Treaty Including the Constitution of the League of States, Adopted by the English 21 Conference of the University of North Carolina* (Chapel Hill, Mar. 28, 1919). A copy of this 18-page pamphlet in the New York Public Library is presumably the only one extant.
22. *TH*, Feb. 14, 1919.
23. AO, p. 34.   24. bMS Am 1883 (1263).
25. Hilton G. West to John S. Terry, Feb. 26, 1947, TW-NcU.
26. *TH*, Mar. 28, 1919.
27. *TH*, Apr. 4, Apr. 18, May 16, 1919; Moses Rountree, "My Recollections of Thomas Wolfe," n.d., typescript, owned by Mrs. Lewis T. Everette, Jr., Goldsboro, N. C.
28. *YY*, 1919, p. 336.   30. AO, p. 34.
29. *TH*, Apr. 4, 1919.   31. *TH*, May 23, 1919.
32. According to E. Earle Rives, Don Bishop notes, TW-NcU.

33. AO, pp. 34–35.   34. Turnbull, p. 20.
35. Foreword, *The Blue Ridge Magazine*. See also *TH*, Jan. 30, 1920.
36. AO, p. 7.   37. AO, p. 9.
38. Ben Cone, Sr., interview, Sept. 17, 1974.
39. Eaton, p. 147.
40. Wolfe to Edwin A. Greenlaw, Oct. [21], 1924, typescript copy, bMS Am 1883.2 (149).
41. Wolfe to Edwin A. Greenlaw, Jan. 28, 1930, typescript copy, bMS Am 1883.2 (149).
42. AO, p. 26.

5. *Junior*

1. William U. Snyder, *Thomas Wolfe: Ulysses and Narcissus* (Athens: Ohio Univ. Press, 1971), pp. 34, 41.
2. AO, pp. 10–11.
3. John B. Mitchell, in *Daily Press* (Newport News-Hampton, Va.), Oct. 26, 1969.
4. *The Letters of Thomas Wolfe to His Mother*, ed. C. Hugh Holman and Sue Fields Ross (Chapel Hill: Univ. of North Carolina Press, 1968), p. 5.
5. AO, p. 12.
6. Mabel Wolfe Wheaton, with LeGette Blythe, *Thomas Wolfe and His Family* (Garden City, N. Y.: Doubleday, 1961), p. 169.
7. Hayden Norwood, *The Marble Man's Wife: Thomas Wolfe's Mother* (New York: Scribner's, 1947), p. 143.
8. *The Letters of Thomas Wolfe to His Mother*, p. 5; John B. Mitchell, in *Daily Press*, Oct. 26, 1969.
9. AO, pp. 13–14.   11. *TH*, Oct. 23, 1918.
10. AO, p. 17.   12. *TH*, Oct. 2, 1918.
13. Clement Eaton, "Student Days with Thomas Wolfe," *Georgia Review*, 17 (1963), 150.
14. *YY*, 1919, unnumbered page.
15. *TH*, June 14, 1919.
16. AO, p. 17; Mrs. Allen G. Gill, interview, Aug. 25, 1975.
17. Francis Dubose Uzzell, interview, June 6, 1976.
18. Forrest G. Miles to Don Bishop, Jan. 16, 1941, typescript copy, TW-NcU.
19. TW-NcU.   20. AO, p. 54.
21. U.N.C. Records office.
22. Hilton G. West to John S. Terry, Feb. 26, 1947, TW-NcU.
23. Forrest G. Miles to Don Bishop, Jan. 16, 1941, typescript copy, TW-NcU.
24. Daniel L. Grant to Don Bishop, Mar. 3, 1941, typescript copy, TW-NcU.
25. *TH*, Nov. 13, 1918.
26. Houston S. Everett to John S. Terry, Apr. 5, 1947, TW-NcU.

27. Forrest G. Miles to Don Bishop, Jan. 16, 1941, typescript copy, TW-NcU.

28. Robert Coleman Gibbs, "Thomas Wolfe's Four Years at Chapel Hill: A Study of Biographical Source Material," Thesis, U.N.C., 1958, p. 45.

29. *TH*, Oct. 9, Oct. 16, 1918, Feb. 14, Apr. 11, 1919.

30. *TH*, Nov. 22, Dec. 13, 1918.   32. AO, p. 24.

31. AO, pp. 17–21.   33. AO, pp. 21–22.

34. John S. Terry, at Thomas Wolfe Biography Club, New York University, May 17, 1947, typescript, TW-NcU.

35. Norwood, pp. 56–57.   36. AO, p. 21.

37. AO, pp. 22–23. Frank P. Graham was a first cousin, not a brother, of President Edward K. Graham.

38. Thomas Wolfe, "Chapel Hill Recollections," ca. 1932, bMS Am 1883 (1172).

39. Dialectic Society minutes, Feb. 7, 1919, Southern Historical Collection, NcU.

40. *TH*, May 23, 1919.

41. W. Edwin Matthews, "Di Society Holds Smoker," typescript, TW-NcU; Dialectic Society minutes, May 24, 1919.

42. *YY*, 1919, unnumbered page.

43. Wolfe, "Chapel Hill Recollections."

44. AO, p. 30.   45. *TH*, Jan. 17, 1919.

46. Thomas Wolfe, in *The Star and Lamp of Pi Kappa Phi*, Mar. 1919, p. 66.

47. *TH*, Feb. 28, 1919.   49. AO, p. 54.

48. *TH*, Feb. 21, 1919.   50. *Notebooks*, II, 853–54.

51. *Charlotte Observer*, Mar. 30, 1941.

52. Andrew Turnbull, *Thomas Wolfe* (New York: Scribner's, 1967), p. 29.

53. AO, p. 48.   54. AO, p. 37.

55. Frederick H. Koch, "Thomas Wolfe—Playmaker," *Carolina Play-Book* (U.N.C.), 8 (1935), 35.

56. Frank P. Graham to John S. Terry, Mar. 17, 1942, TW-NcU.

57. J. E. Dowd to Don Bishop, Jan. 14, 1941, typescript copy, TW-NcU.

58. LeGette Blythe and Ernest Neiman, tape (NcU) of Wolfe reminiscences at a dinner, Chapel Hill, Dec. 5, 1958.

59. Hilton G. West to John S. Terry, Feb. 26, 1947, TW-NcU.

60. AO, pp. 52–53.

61. LeGette Blythe, "The Thomas Wolfe I Knew," *Saturday Review of Literature*, Aug. 25, 1945, p. 19.

62. William H. Bobbitt, interview, Dec. 7, 1973.

63. Joel Brooks, in *Asheville Citizen-Times*, Dec. 31, 1950.

64. Hilton G. West to John S. Terry, Feb. 26, 1947, TW-NcU.

65. AO, p. 24.

66. According to Nathan Mobley, Don Bishop notes, TW-NcU.

67. Koch, p. 35.

68. Terry papers, handwritten note, TW-NcU.

69. AO, p. 34.

70. E. Earle Rives to Don Bishop, Feb. 14, 1941, typescript copy. TW-NcU.

71. Don Bishop, "Thomas Wolfe," *Car. Mag.*, Mar. 1942, p. 35.

72. Donnell Van Noppen to Don Bishop, Feb. 6, 1941, typescript copy, TW-NcU.

73. Elizabeth Lay (Mrs. Paul) Green, tape (NcU) of Wolfe reminiscences at a dinner, Chapel Hill, Dec. 5, 1958.

74. According to Nathan Mobley, Don Bishop notes, TW-NcU.

75. *Car. Mag.*, Apr. 1919, pp. 68–69.   76. *Letters*, p. 554.

77. William H. Bobbitt, interview, Dec. 7, 1973.

78. Bishop, p. 35.

79. Jim Schlosser, in *Raleigh Times*, May 21, 1966.

80. We have been smoke; i. e., those days of youth are gone like smoke.

81. AO, pp. 32, 37, 34, 52, 35, 23, 52, 47, 24.

82. *TH*, Apr. 11, 1919; Y.M.C.A. *Handbook of the University of North Carolina, 1918–1919*, p. 39.

83. *YY*, 1919, unnumbered pages.

84. *Handbook, 1918–1919*, p. 28.   85. *TH*, Mar. 14, 1919.

86. LeGette Blythe, in *Charlotte Observer*, Oct. 14, 1945.

87. Hilton G. West to John S. Terry, Feb. 26, 1947, TW-NcU.

88. *TH*, Mar. 7, 1919.

89. Moses Rountree to Richard Walser, Dec. 4, 1974.

90. *TH*, Mar. 28, 1919.   91. *TH*, Apr. 11, 1919.

92. John S. Terry, "Wolfe Collection Criticism" folder, also untitled folder, typescript, TW-NcU.

93. *TH*, Apr. 18, 1919.   95. *TH*, May 2, 1919.

94. bMS Am 1883 (1259).   96. AO, pp. 31–32.

97. Fred Moore to Richard Walser, Feb. 17, 1975.

98. According to Nathan Mobley, Don Bishop notes, TW-NcU.

99. Donnell Van Noppen to Don Bishop, Feb. 6, 1941, typescript copy, TW-NcU.

100. Sam Ragan, in *News and Observer* (Raleigh), Aug. 20, 1967.

101. *The Star and Lamp of Pi Kappa Phi*, Mar. 1919, p. 66; Apr. 1919, p. 104.

102. Bishop, p. 35.   104. *TH*, May 2, 1919.

103. Eaton, p. 151.   105. AO, p. 24.

106. LeGette Blythe to Don Bishop, Feb. 10, 1941, typescript copy, TW-NcU.

107. *TH*, May 30, 1919.   108. U.N.C. Records office.

109. Thomas Wolfe, *The Crisis in Industry* (Chapel Hill: Published by the University, 1919), pp. [3], 11, 8, 10.

110. Richard S. Kennedy, *The Window of Memory: The Literary Career of Thomas Wolfe* (Chapel Hill: Univ. of North Carolina Press, 1962), p. 54.

111. Helen K. Landon to Mabel Wolfe Wheaton, Sept. 29, 1940, TW-NcU.

112. George R. Preston, Jr., *Thomas Wolfe: A Bibliography* (New York: Charles S. Boesen, 1943), p. 19.

6. *Proff Koch*

1. Samuel Selden and Mary Tom Sphangos, *Frederick H. Koch: Pioneer Playmaker* (Chapel Hill: Univ. of North Carolina Library, 1954), p. 11.

2. *TH*, Dec. 9, 1916.   3. *TH*, May 5, 1917.

4. F. H. K. [Frederick Henry Koch], "Thomas Wolfe—Playmaker," *Carolina Play-Book* (U.N.C.), 8 (1935), 35.

5. Thomas Wolfe, "The Man Who Lives with His Idea," *Carolina Play-Book* (U.N.C.), 16 (1943), 18–19, 15.

6. Archibald Henderson, "Thomas Wolfe: Play Maker," *Carolina Play-Book* (U.N.C.), 16 (1943), 28.

7. *TH*, Oct. 16, 1918.   8. AO, p. 32.

9. Thomas Wolfe, "A Previously Unpublished Statement by Thomas Wolfe," *Carolina Quarterly* (U.N.C.), 11 (Spring 1960), 9.

10. *Notebooks*, I, 61.

11. Richard S. Kennedy, *The Window of Memory: The Literary Career of Thomas Wolfe* (Chapel Hill: Univ. of North Carolina Press, 1962), p. 48.

12. Andrew Turnbull, *Thomas Wolfe* (New York: Scribner's, 1967), p. 328, n. 7.

13. bMS Am 1883 (1307), folder 6.

14. Thomas Wolfe, foreword to "The Return of Buck Gavin," typescript of original holograph manuscript, Carolina Playmakers Scrapbook (NcU), 1 (1918–19), 32b.

15. Mabel Wheaton Wolfe, with LeGette Blythe, *Thomas Wolfe and His Family* (Garden City, N. Y.: Doubleday, 1961), p. 80.

16. Frequently reprinted since its first appearance in Frederick H. Koch, ed., *Carolina Folk-Plays*, Second Series (New York: Henry Holt, 1924).

17. Wolfe to Frederick H. Koch, ca. June 1924, Carolina Playmakers Scrapbook (NcU), 2 (1920–21 [*sic*]), 199.

18. C. Hugh Holman, in Paschal Reeves, ed., *Thomas Wolfe and the Glass of Time* (Athens: Univ. of Georgia Press, 1971), p. 134.

19. Wheaton, p. 190.   22. *TH*, Jan. 17, 1919.

20. AO, pp. 32–33.   23. *TH*, Feb. 28, 1919.

21. *TH*, Dec. 6, 1918.   24. *TH*, Mar. 7, 1919.

25. *TH*, Apr. 11, 1919.

26. LeGette Blythe, "About Tom Wolfe," *The Miscellany* (Davidson College), Dec. 1966, p. 44.

27. LeGette Blythe, "The Merry Little Man in the Norfolk Jacket," *Carolina Play-Book* (U.N.C.), 8 (1935), 60.

28. Moses Rountree, "My Recollections of Thomas Wolfe," n.d., typescript, owned by Mrs. Lewis T. Everette, Jr., Goldsboro, N. C.

29. F. H. K. [Frederick Henry Koch], p. 36.

30. Alden Stahr, "Thomas Wolfe at Chapel Hill," *Car. Mag.*, Apr. 24, 1932, p. 1.

31. "Mrs. Leavitt Dies Sunday," *News and Observer* (Raleigh), Mar. 23, 1964.

32. Program, *Original Folk Plays* (broadside), Mar. 14 and 15, 1919, TW-NcU.

33. Archibald Henderson, in *Charlotte Observer*, Mar. 30, 1941.

34. "Original Folk Plays Presented," *News and Observer* (Raleigh), Mar. 16, 1919.

35. According to Nathan Mobley, Don Bishop notes, TW-NcU.

36. Henderson, "Thomas Wolfe: Play Maker," p. 28; Archibald Henderson, in *Charlotte Observer*, Mar. 16, 1919.

37. Ann Preston Bridgers, "Thomas Wolfe: Legends of a Man's Hunger in His Youth," *Saturday Review of Literature*, Apr. 6, 1935, p. 599.

38. *TH*, Mar. 28, 1919.   39. Stahr, p. 8.

40. "Thomas Wolfe Dies . . . ," *News and Observer* (Raleigh), Sept. 16, 1938.

41. AO, p. 33.   44. bMS Am 1883 (18)(19).

42. bMS Am 1883 (15).   45. Family papers, TW-NcU.

43. bMS Am 1883 (10).   46. Family papers, TW-NcU.

47. bMS Am 1883 (16)(17).

48. bMS Am 1883 (20). See also Pat M. Ryan, Introduction to Thomas Wolfe, *The Mountains* (Chapel Hill: Univ. of North Carolina Press, 1970).

49. *TH*, June 14, 1919.

50. "As They Recall Thomas Wolfe," *Southern Packet* (Asheville), Apr. 1948, p. 4.

51. Carolina *Play-Book* (U.N.C.), 9 (1938), 70–75. Reprinted in Frederick H. Koch, ed., *Carolina Folk-Plays* (New York: Henry Holt, 1941), pp. 127–43.

52. Frederick J. Cohn, interview, July 2, 1974.

53. Arthur S. Harris, Jr., "Thomas Wolfe's One Great Book," *World in Books* (Boston), Sept. 1946, p. 5.

54. "A Previously Unpublished Statement by Thomas Wolfe," p. 10.

55. *TH*, Mar. 18, 1920. In Carolina Playmakers Scrapbook (NcU), 1:108, there is a handwritten notation, probably by Koch, that this "Bibliograph" is "by T. C. W."

7. *Senior*

1. Mabel Wolfe Wheaton, with LeGette Blythe, *Thomas Wolfe and His Family* (Garden City, N. Y.: Doubleday, 1961), pp. 183–84.

2. Philip Clark, in *Asheville Citizen*, June 2, 1959; Andrew Turnbull, *Thomas Wolfe* (New York: Scribner's, 1967), p. 34.

3. Note by Lora French attached to a post card sent her by Wolfe postmarked from Anderson, S. C., Aug. 11, 1919, TW-NcU.

4. *TH*, Dec. 13, 1919.   5. *TH*, Oct. 11, 1919.

6. *The Letters of Thomas Wolfe to His Mother*, ed. C. Hugh Holman and Sue Fields Ross (Chapel Hill: Univ. of North Carolina Press, 1968), p. 6.

7. Richard H. Thornton to John S. Terry, Sept. 26, 1950, TW-NcU.

8. Albert Coates, interview, Dec. 4, 1973.

9. Addison Hibbard to Don Bishop, Feb. 20, 1941, typescript copy, TW-NcU.

10. *TH*, July 20, 1920; Richard Walser, "Editor Who Threw Out the Ads," *State* (Raleigh), Jan. 1, 1972, p. 14.

11. Wolfe to George [George Denny?], Feb. 10, 1921, TW-NcU.

12. Julia [Mrs. Corydon P.] Spruill, interview, Nov. 14, 1973.

13. AO, pp. 51–52.   14. *TH*, Oct. 11, 1919.

15. According to Ben Cone, Sr., in Pocahontas Wight Edmunds, *Tar Heels Track the Century* (Raleigh: Edwards & Broughton, 1966), p. 268.

16. *Y.Y.*, 1920, p. 49.

17. Don Bishop, in *Greensboro Daily News*, May 10, 1953.

18. C. R. Sumner, in *Asheville Citizen-Times*, Nov. 19, 1950; Paul Green, interview, July 18, 1968.

19. Dialectic Society minutes, Oct. 18, Oct. 25, Nov. 15, 1919; Jan. 31, 1920, Southern Historical Collection, NcU.

20. *TH*, Oct. 25, 1919.

21. *Tar Baby* (U.N.C.), Nov. 18, 1919, pp. 4–5; reprinted in *A Century of College Humor*, ed. Dan Carlinsky (New York: Random House, 1971), pp. 52–53.

22. According to Corydon P. Spruill, Don Bishop notes, TW-NcU.

23. Hilton G. West to John S. Terry, Feb. 26, 1947, TW-NcU.

24. According to Ben Cone, Sr., Don Bishop notes, TW-NcU.

25. According to W. R. Berryhill, Don Bishop notes, TW-NcU.

26. According to W. H. Andrews, Jr., Don Bishop notes, TW-NcU.

27. Alden Stahr, "Thomas Wolfe at Chapel Hill," *Car. Mag.*, Apr. 24, 1932, p. 8.

28. bMS Am 1883 (160).   29. *TH*, Nov. 15, 1919.

30. *TH*, Oct. 11, Oct. 18, Oct. 25, Nov. 1, Nov. 22, Dec. 13, 1919.

31. *The Letters of Thomas Wolfe to His Mother*, p. 7.

32. Turnbull, p. 35.

33. Walser, pp. 13–14; *TH*, Nov. 27, 1919.

34. Ernest Seeman to John S. Terry, [Aug. 6, 1951], TW-NcU.

35. J. Jerome Pence to John S. Terry, Mar. 19, 1947, TW-NcU.

36. *TH*, Nov. 22, Nov. 27, Dec. 6, 1919.

37. *TH*, Dec. 13, 1919.

38. Richard Walser, "An Early Wolfe Essay—and the Downfall of a Hero," *Modern Fiction Studies*, 11 (1965), 269–74.

39. *The Letters of Thomas Wolfe to His Mother*, p. 7.

40. Donnell Van Noppen to Don Bishop, Feb. 6, 1941, typescript copy, TW-NcU.

41. *The Letters of Thomas Wolfe to His Mother*, p. 7.

42. Pete Ivey, in *Raleigh Times*, Nov. 4, 1965.

43. Clement Eaton, "Student Days with Thomas Wolfe," *Georgia Review*, 17 (1963), 146.

44. Ransom Gurganus, "Thomas Wolfe: Undergraduate," *Washington Square Critic* (New York University), May 1935, p. 2.

45. According to William T. Polk, Don Bishop notes, TW-NcU.

46. C. R. Sumner, untitled radio program, n. d., p. 5, typescript, Thomas Wolfe Collection, Pack Memorial Library, Asheville.

47. Corydon P. Spruill, interview, Nov. 14, 1973.

48. "Doings of a Carolina Man," probably by Wolfe, *TH*, Feb. 14, 1920; "With Apologies to Pepys," also probably by Wolfe, *TH*, Feb. 28, 1920; *Tar Baby* (U.N.C.), Mar. 13, 1920, p. 15; *TH*, Feb. 21, 1920.

49. *YY*, 1920, p. 50.

50. *Thomas Wolfe's Purdue Speech "Writing and Living,"* ed. William Braswell and Leslie A. Field ([West Lafayette, Ind.]: Purdue Univ. Studies, 1964), p. 33.

51. *Letters*, p. 192.

52. AO, pp. 26–27, 50, 45.

53. AO, pp. 30, 52.

54. *TH*, Apr. 2, 1920.

55. AO, p. 45.

56. Printed program (broadside), TW-NcU.

57. *TH*, Mar. 13, 1920.

58. *TH*, Mar. 27, 1920.

59. According to Frank P. Graham, Don Bishop notes, TW-NcU; *State* (Raleigh), Jan. 11, 1958, p. 16.

60. Wolfe to Archibald Henderson, Oct. 7, 1924, TW-NcU.

61. *TH*, Jan. 23, Jan. 30, Feb. 7, Feb. 14, Mar. 13, Apr. 2, Apr. 24, May 8, May 15, 1920.

62. Paul Green, interview, Dec. 4, 1973.

63. [Tom Bost], "Not Machine, but Man," *Greensboro Daily News*, Feb. 9, 1947.

64. *TH*, Feb. 28, 1920.

65. Lenoir Chambers, in *News and Observer* (Raleigh), May 2, 1920; Pete Ivey, "Tommy Wolfe's School Days," *State* (Raleigh), May 25, 1935, p. 9.

66. *TH*, Mar. 13, 1920.

67. *TH*, May 29, 1920.

68. *Tar Baby* (U.N.C.), Dec. 2, 1919, p. 12; Jan. 29, 1920, p. 8.

69. Elizabeth Nowell, *Thomas Wolfe* (Garden City, N. Y.: Doubleday, 1960), p. 39.

70. *Tar Baby* (U.N.C.), Apr. 10, 1920, p. 39.

71. *Letters*, p. 8.

72. Ben Dixon MacNeill, in *News and Observer* (Raleigh), Nov. 12, 1950.

73. Lenoir Chambers, in *News and Observer* (Raleigh), May 2, 1920.

74. Don Bishop notes, TW-NcU; *YY*, 1920, p. 372; *TH*, Nov. 15, 1919, Mar. 27, 1920.

75. *TH*, May 8, May 15, 1920.

76. *TH*, May 8, May 29, 1920.

77. *Purdue Speech*, p. 39.

78. "As They Recall Thomas Wolfe," *Southern Packet* (Asheville), Apr. 1948, p. 4.

79. Wolfe to Milton A. Abernethy, Apr. 15, 1932, TW-NcU.

80. *The Letters of Thomas Wolfe to His Mother*, p. 12.

81. *Purdue Speech*, p. 39.

82. *TH*, June 5, 1920.

83. *YY*, 1920, p. 52.

84. According to Nathan Mobley, Don Bishop notes, TW-NcU.

85. *YY*, 1920, p. 103.

86. Fred Wolfe to Wolfe, May 22, 1920, typescript copy, TW-NcU.

87. Wheaton, p. 195.   88. AO, p. 56.

89. *Program: Senior Class Day* (brochure), TW-NcU.

90. *YY*, 1920, p. 51.

91. According To Frank P. Graham, Don Bishop notes, TW-NcU; "As They Recall Thomas Wolfe," p. 9.

92. Wheaton, p. 194; *TH*, July 20, 1920; commencement invitation (brochure), TW-NcU.

93. *Letters*, p. 8.

94. Jonathan Daniels, *Thomas Wolfe: October Recollections* (Columbia, S. C.: Bostic & Thornley, 1961), p. 10.

8. Horace Williams

1. Thomas Clark Pollock and Oscar Cargill, *Thomas Wolfe at Washington Square* (New York: New York Univ. Press, 1954), p. 16.

2. AO, pp. 8–9.

3. Clement Eaton, "Student Days with Thomas Wolfe," *Georgia Review*, 17 (1963), 148.

4. AO, pp. 26, 39.   5. Eaton, p. 149.

6. Wolfe to Horace Williams, probably never mailed, ca. 1923, bMS Am 1883.2 (374).

7. AO, pp. 44–45.

8. Robert Watson Winston, *Horace Williams: Gadfly of Chapel Hill* (Chapel Hill: Univ. of North Carolina Press, 1942), p. 57.

9. Robert B. House, *The Light That Shines: Chapel Hill, 1912–1916* (Chapel Hill: Univ. of North Carolina Press, 1964), p. 87.

10. Winston, p. 55.   11. House, p. 88.

12. According to W. H. Berryhill, Don Bishop notes, TW-NcU.

13. Henry Horace Williams, *Logic for Living: Lectures of 1921–22*, ed. Jane Ross Hammer (New York: Philosophical Library, 1951), p. 153.

14. Julia Canady, in *Smithfield* (N. C.) *Herald*, Dec. 15, 1953.

15. AO, p. 45.

16. *Thomas Wolfe's Purdue Speech "Writing and Living,"* ed. William Braswell and Leslie A. Field ([West Lafayette, Ind.]: Purdue Univ. Studies, 1964), p. 32.

17. *TH*, Sept. 30, 1916.   21. *Notebooks*, II, 857.

18. AO, p. 39.   22. Winston, p. 72.

19. *Purdue Speech*, pp. 33–34.   23. Winston, p. 133.

20. AO, p. 39.   24. AO, pp. 40–41.

25. William H. Bobbitt, interview, Dec. 7, 1973.

26. AO, p. 39.

27. According to E. Earle Rives, Don Bishop notes, TW-NcU.

28. AO, pp. 40–42. 29. AO, p. 55.

30. Henry Horace Williams, *The Education of Horace Williams* (Chapel Hill: Author, 1936), pp. 129, 192, 188, 195.

31. AO, p. 44.

32. Louis R. Wilson, *The University of North Carolina, 1900–1930* (Chapel Hill: Univ. of North Carolina Press, 1957), p. 505.

33. bMS Am 1883 (54)(55).

34. *Letters*, p. 18. 35. Winston, pp. 37–39.

36. William H. Bobbitt, interview, Dec. 7, 1973.

37. *Letters*, p. 104.

38. Williams, *Logic for Living*, pp. 23–24.

39. *The Education of Horace Williams*, p. 122.

40. Williams, *Logic for Living*, p. 231.

41. S. F. Telfair, Jr., "The Triangle," *Car. Mag.*, Jan. 1917, p. 143.

42. William H. Bobbitt, interview, Dec. 7, 1973.

43. AO, p. 42.

44. William H. Bobbitt, interview, May 2, 1972.

45. Edgar Emmett Stanton, Jr., "Hegel and Thomas Wolfe," Diss. Florida State, 1960, explores the Hegelian influence on Wolfe's mature fiction. See also C. Hugh Holman, *The Loneliness at the Core: Studies in Thomas Wolfe* (Baton Rouge: Louisiana State Univ. Press, 1975) pp. 6–7; and Richard S. Kennedy, *The Window of Memory: The Literary Career of Thomas Wolfe* (Chapel Hill: Univ. of North Carolina Press, 1962), pp. 49–53.

46. AO, pp. 37–38.

47. Williams, *Logic for Living*, pp. 44, 105, 109.

48. *The Education of Horace Williams*, p. 123.

49. Williams, *Logic for Living*, p. 275; *The Education of Horace Williams*, p. 55.

50. *Purdue Speech*, pp. 34–35. 51. AO, p. 40.

52. AO, p. 56. See also *Notebooks*, I, 132.

Appendix: Dramatic Fragment about Horace Williams

1. Professor Weldon is voted a Baldwin Professorship, TW-NcU.

2. bMS Am 1883 (63). 3. bMS Am 1883 (64).

4. bMS Am 1883 (54)(55). See chap. 8, n. 33.

5. Professor Homer Weldon and his tenant George Sparrow, TW-NcU; "The Old School" (Wolfe's title), conversation between a man and his wife, bMS Am 1883 (60).

6. Professor Weldon is told he has cancer, bMS Am 1883 (56); about Professor Weldon's operation, bMS Am 1883 (57); about the posthumous publication of Professor Weldon's diary, bMS Am 1883 (59); after Professor Weldon's death, a proposal is made to write his biography, bMS Am 1883 (62).

7. Professor Wilson and a student named Ramsay, TW-NcU; the professor and a former student named Reeves, TW-NcU; Professor Weldon gives a

student advice about women, bMS Am 1883 (56); about Professor Weldon's possible successor, bMS Am 1883 (58); Professor Weldon's conversations with two students, bMS Am 1883 (61).

8. About Professor Baggett and university appropriations, TW-NcU; Professor Weldon is voted a Baldwin Professorship, TW-NcU (see n. 1 above); Professor Weldon is ostracized at a faculty meeting, TW-NcU; Professor Weldon on "Principle," TW-NcU; prose account of contrast between Mr. W. [Williams] and Professor X [Greenlaw], bMS Am 1883 (54)(55) (see n. 4 above); visit of several important faculty members to Professor Weldon, bMS Am 1883 (56); faculty meeting at which Professor Weldon is harshly criticized, bMS Am 1883 (65).

9. *Notebooks,* I, 18–20.

10. bMS Am 1883 (59). See third item in n. 6 above.

11. *Letters,* pp. 35–38.

12. TW-NcU. See first item in n. 7 above.

Index

pranks, 15, 36–37, 75, 79, 82–84, 92, 102, 111
Pratt, Joseph Hyde, 73
Presbyterian church, 11, 107
Princeton University, 5, 13, 34
problem novel, 60–61, 96
Price, Lillian, 52
psychology, 37, 130
Purefoy, Dr. George W., 45
Purrington, A. L., 67
Raleigh, 5, 6, 7, 16, 23, 31, 34, 35, 40, 42, 52, 83, 111, 115, 116, 117, 118
Raleigh Street, 28
Range Finder, 61
Rankin, Edgar R., 6
Ransom, W. E., 22
religion, 11, 21, 77, 83, 110, 126, 132
Reynolds, N. A., 45
Richmond, Va., 17, 63, 64, 107
Riverside Park, 34
Rives, E. Earle, 76
Roberts, J. M., 3, 6
Roberts, Margaret, 3, 4, 5, 6, 33, 38, 54, 55
Rondthaler, T. E., 50, 79
rooms and lodging, 7, 15, 16, 19, 35, 43, 65–66, 82, 101, 108
Ross, Marion, 9, 11
Rountree, Moses, 58, 92–93, 103, 142
St. Mary's College, 42
S.A.T.C. *See* Student Army Training Corps
Satyrs, 78, 87, 111
Science of Thought, The, 131
Seeman, Ernest, 67, 106
sexual experiences, 18, 21, 23, 32, 52, 69, 110–11
Shakespeare, William, 4, 50, 55–56, 87, 88–89, 92, 106
Shaw, George Bernard, 50, 60, 87, 88–89, 112
short stories, undergraduate, 50, 87, 104. *See also* short story by Wolfe
short story by Wolfe, 44–45
Sigma Upsilon, 50, 102
Smith, Mamie, 18

Smith Hall, 7
smokers. *See* banquets, smokers, and stunt nights
Sophomore Debate, 44
Sophomore-Freshman debating team, 20
Sorrell, W. B., 73
South building, 7, 11, 35, 39, 72
Sparrow, Jack, 8
Sparrow, Minnie, 91
Spaugh, R. A., 59
speaking. *See* debate, declamation, and speaking
Spruill, Corydon P., 47, 78, 84, 100, 109, 111, 122, 142
Spruill, Julia, 142
Stacy, Marvin H., 11, 70
State Normal School (Greensboro), 38
Statesville, 65
Station Hotel, 111
Strowd's Hill, 107
Student Army Training Corps, 65, 68, 70, 72, 73, 86, 127
Student Council, 37, 102, 121, 122
Stunt Night, 81, 84. *See also* banquets, smokers, and stunt nights
stunt nights. *See* banquets, smokers, and stunt nights
Sumner, C. R., 109
Swain Hall, 7, 9, 16, 40, 43, 70, 73, 77, 107, 109, 111
Tar Baby. See *Carolina Tar Baby*
Tar Heel, The, 14, 22, 24, 40, 44, 51, 58, 66, 67, 68, 73, 76, 78, 82, 84, 87, 92, 100, 101, 103, 104–8, 109, 113, 115, 118, 143
Tar Heel Tavern, 18
Tennent, Charles G. (Buzz), 13, 142
Tennent, George Raby, 18, 47, 142
Tennessee, University of, 4
Terry, John Skally, 19, 20–21, 32, 38, 45, 47, 49, 50, 51, 56, 67, 69–70, 71, 76, 81, 103, 122, 142
themes, compositions, and essays by